Bitcoin Digital Law

Why Cryptocurrencies are Digital Laws of the Internet Jurisdiction and Why States Must Adapt

Ignacio J. Ferrer-Bonsoms Hernández

Contents

PROLOGUE

Ready Player Two: Society Is Different in the Virtual World

"We, who are as much as you, but together are more than you, make you principal, king, and lord among equals, provided that you uphold our privileges and liberties; and if not, then no."

– Formula of the oath of the kings of Aragon.

Once upon a time, everything turned on virtue. Virtue in a nutshell. A person was either good or bad, and the inner world showed through the outer one: "By their works ye shall know them" (Matthew 7:15).

In the final decades of the last century, however, the Internet arrived, and God allowed another world to become possible for human beings: the virtual world.

In the virtual world and in the real one, virtue is the same because morality is the same. Human nature does not change, but society does. In a virtual society, communities can create worlds that feel real even though they do not exist in physical space.

That is what God made possible: the human being, created in His image and likeness, is also a creator. Yet, He did not change the rules of morality. What counts as good or evil is the same here as there.

However, the realities themselves differ. One world is physical, created by God. The other is virtual, created by human beings. Killing a person is not the same as playing Assassin's Creed or Call of Duty.

As with movies, the moral rules are those of the viewer, yet everyone understands they are watching a story told with images. Cowboy gunfire and the swords of the three musketeers do not kill.

Movies were eventually surpassed by the Internet. What the Internet has achieved is to make the virtual world part of everyday reality. The world created by human beings now constantly interacts with the world created by God because people are present in both at the same time.

The change brought by the Internet is not only technological. We have learned to live inside the virtual world, almost as if we had stepped inside the movie. The virtual world has become a space where we work, love, argue, buy, and sell, and it is now a piece of reality we carry in our pockets.

In the virtual world, moral rules remain intact, but social rules are rewritten. We are facing a new kind of law because we are facing a new kind of society, full of unexpected communities. These communities are constantly being created and reshaped. They are full of life and, at the same time, always one click away from disappearing, both virtually and in their real economic or political consequences.

When the network was born, legal rules were reduced to domain names and little else. Once a domain name was registered, it had to be filled. The important thing was the domain.

Soon, the fights stopped being about names and became about content. Around the year 2000, the Internet was a world of portals that had to be filled with content. The goal was to gather information so that the user would stay there, without leaving the domain, consuming advertising and buying products in that store. The more on the same site, the better. Traffic was generated by aggregation. Portals were like large shopping malls that sold almost everything.

Then Google came along. Portals were no longer necessary because a free search engine appeared that could find everything word by word. It did not matter what the domain was, or whether the website was big or small. The user, without paying anything for the comparison, could choose what seemed to offer the best quality. Someone sitting in Mexico City could buy from a small store in Jaca (Barrabés, Spain) as easily as from a multinational chain. The center of gravity moved from who owned the portal to who provided the most useful answer.

Google's success was also possible because society invested in incredible hardware improvements for the Internet, from modems to fiber optics, to 3G, to 4G, and now 5G, everywhere in the world, all within a very short time. So not only could texts be shared, but also images and videos (YouTube) in high resolution and at very high transmission speeds.

A free and extraordinarily productive universe was born around Google: email (free), calendar (free), contacts (free), spreadsheets (free), documents (free), and many other tools. It was a chromatic scale of productive gratuity that captivated young people. It worked beautifully, because it was free. In reality, it was paid for with data and by consenting to targeted advertising. The model wiped out much of the competition and created a giant that organizes a good part of the world's information.

The first world community was created around Wisdom, which proved to be "omnibus mobilibus mobilior": "Wisdom surpasses all movement in mobility; she passes through and penetrates everything by virtue of her purity. It is a breath of the power of God, a pure emanation of the glory of the Almighty, so that nothing tainted can reach it" (Wisdom VII, 24–25).

Thanks to Wisdom, human beings have created virtual as well as real communities of all types and origins: from Linux users to online poker players or LibreOffice developers, not to mention the deep web or ransomware criminals. People who do not know each other at all create a community, and many communities together create a society, with all the good and all the bad of the human soul. That is one of Ignacio Ferrer-Bonsoms' theses in this book.

The real Internet communities are not those born around centralized systems. No genuine Internet community is created by socialism. The users of a bank, whatever it is, do not form an Internet community.

Nor do the "online" students of a distance-learning university.

Their community is imposed on them and is therefore centralized and organized by a third party. There is no real equality in those communities because they are not Internet communities at all, but groups imposed by power in which one does not join voluntarily but out of necessity. There is always a network administrator who has all the power.

On the Internet, the only true communities are peer-to-peer. They are communities of equals. They are, in a way, communes, assemblies of people, free or paid, in which, once the rules have been created, you can join or not, because joining is voluntary and leaving is also voluntary.

When you are in, everyone has all the information, and everyone has equal opportunities. They do not all have the same productivity, but they do have the same opportunities.

The paradigm is Napster, BitTorrent, or eMule. There are many more. No one will ever be able to beat them, because in the virtual world, power is much more democratic than in the real world, precisely because it has been created from below, not from above.

Satoshi Nakamoto fused the peer-to-peer model with cryptology and created Bitcoin, which is nothing more than a peer-to-peer electronic cash system. It is the main enemy of banking and classical monetary institutions because it dispenses with all financial intermediaries. Bitcoin is a purely peer-to-peer version of electronic money that allows people to make payments directly between one another without going through a financial institution.

It took time to catch on. Today, it is the present of the new economy: the currency used for payments in virtual reality is overtaking all other fiat money systems in value, because it is transparent, contains no cheating, is self-managed, and is cheaper than any traditional currency.

Freedom is also built with money, and if peer-to-peer users wanted freedom, they needed a monetary asset. They have had it for a long time. Now they use it. And no one will be able to stop them, because in a democratic society, initiatives are born from below and so are regulations.

What is imposed from above without respecting the freedom of exchange to keep what belongs to others is not democratic. It is socialism, a crude form of stealing that consists of legalizing theft through the budget.

Users of peer-to-peer systems now have much more than Bitcoin. With new "tokens," they have the possibility of exchanging non-monetary assets embedded in electronic blocks in whose transaction no trusted third party intervenes, either, because there is no need. Trust is in the technology itself. The blockchain is more secure than the notarial protocol. Notaries are no longer necessary. Not in the virtual world. Not in the peer-to-peer world.

That is lethal to classical ways of thinking because the peer-to-peer world is already a real world. Anyone who wants to live in the virtual world, which they can enter because virtual reality already exists, can enrich themselves in crypto assets. The user of decentralized peer-to-peer networks escapes Leviathan's control.

While it is true that the devil will always be there stalking him, he will have to disguise himself differently. He will no longer be able to present himself as the State, the Bank, the AEAT[1], the DGT[2], the European Union, the IRS, or any other form of abuse of some over others, with the excuse that power was earned in an election.

In the virtual world, all are equal and are organized by communities whose democracy is built in an assembly way, not in a representative way. Each community makes its own laws. Conventional political societies are already living on borrowed time.

A new political theory of freedom is needed, and Ignacio Ferrer-Bonsoms has begun to write it. Socialist equality is over. We will no longer all be equal subjects. The equality of equals has arrived: we will all be equally free. We will see whether we are still allowed to live there when we try to exchange assets from one world to another.

I met Ignacio as I have met, for many years, all my "new people": working. He is a lawyer, like me, and he

---

[1] The Agencia Estatal de Administración Tributaria (AET) is in charge of getting people to pay their taxes in Spain (note from the translator).

[2] The Directorate-General for Traffic (DGT) is the authority responsible for issuing driving licenses in Spain (note from the translator).

was interested in creating an arbitration court for crypto assets. I know quite a bit about arbitration, and at the time, I knew nothing about cryptos. That rejuvenated me because Ignacio is the son of one of my friends. By age, I could be his father.

We combined experiences and out of BACS, which he founded, came BACSIT. Just like Bitcoin, BACSIT is nothing today. We will see in the future. Terra was made with Telefónica's money, and you see what happened. It is the startups that have succeeded. El Corte Inglés or Banco Santander conceive the Internet as a way to save costs. We conceive El Corte Inglés or Banco Santander as a way of incurring costs.

The book you have in your hands is an essay, but also a manual. It is an explanation, as brief as it is useful, first of the genesis of the Internet and then of what Ignacio calls each "law of the Internet," that is, each cryptocurrency. It is meant both for those who are just arriving in this world and for those who already operate in it but need a clearer legal map.

Personally, I have found in the book many personal aids that Ignacio had already provided me through his lessons and classes. For me, already a sexagenarian but still eagerly asking God for more wisdom, meeting Ignacio has been very important.

It has highlighted for me that if I first missed the dot com bubble, then I missed GitHub. Then, I was slow to join Google because I stubbornly stayed in the Microsoft community. I have missed Linux too. Now, I am still in time to join the blockchain communities, where the future of all social and economic life undoubtedly lies.

The Internet is a decentralized jurisdiction in which the rules are set by the programmer, not by a political assembly of representatives. Nothing could be more democratic, because representation is direct, never delegated, and freedom is guaranteed.

If you want to enter a certain sphere of the virtual world, you enter, and if you do not want to, you do not enter. Since one indeed learns by analogy, an idea that Ignacio develops in a whole chapter, I add that you should not miss the movie Ready Player One.

Soon there will be two worlds: the real one in the cloud, which is the one that counts, and the medieval one that counts for nothing, where you still use your ID card and where it does not matter if you are poor in the real world. Everyone will want to live in the virtual world.

As Ignacio says, "In the Internet Jurisdiction, anyone can issue Digital Laws, without the need to belong to a political party, government, or State. In legal, political, and economic terms, Bitcoin is a wild revolution.

For the Digital Laws of the Internet, the concept of community replaces the idea of 'people' in Rousseau's conception of the social contract. In the jurisdiction of the Internet, sovereignty is not local; it is universal." And it is personal, not delegated. There are no politicians. There is only you. That is why they want to kill it.

We will win the battle because "the State can only target Bitcoin in its own territory, but not in the Internet Jurisdiction. Bitcoin could have been defeated at the beginning of its life, in 2009 and the following years, when it barely had nodes supporting its system. But as the community grew, Bitcoin became sovereign and unbreakable."

The law of the new virtual world is still being written. Ignacio prophesies how it will be, or rather describes how it already is. Without quoting himself, he quotes Hayek and returns to Savigny: "Let us not forget that society and not the State is the creator and bearer of Law. It should be remembered that it is society that endorses the political organization of the State, and not the other way around.

Digital Laws do not emanate from above by a central power, but from the very basis of society, called community." The new rules are rules of self-regulation. Nothing could be more perfect, until the oppressive State destroys the freedom of the citizen to live and be happy in a virtual world, where laws are not only non-derogable but also inexorably enforced by code.

There is no need for judges. The machine already judges.

Please read the book because "new markets are often reserved for a select few." Embrace the independence of those who produce, build, and code. "A Central Bank criticizing Bitcoin technology is like a letter carrier ranting because email is not supported on paper." The new productivity is far from contemporary political power.

The new revolution will not be made by the poor. It is being made by productive citizens. And in this new world, you do not simply enter because citizenship is not granted by a passport, but earned by assuming the new rules of each community and accepting the responsibility that comes with that freedom.

Íñigo Coello de Portugal Martínez del Peral,
Senior Counsel of the Council of State in Spain

INTRODUCTION

We are living in a time of great political, technical, and cultural changes throughout the world. Faced with this panorama, some see the glass as half empty. Some people live in fear of what they consider to be the end of time.

Others see nothing and simply go with the flow. Yet some see the glass as half full. They know that from great changes come great opportunities. Despite going against the tide, despite the many difficulties they face and the risks they run, they know that life offers them a chance to try to change the world for the better.

The Internet will be considered one of the great revolutions of history. We are not yet aware of all the effects it will have in the coming years. At the moment, it is difficult for us to predict what the world will be like in twenty years.

Our most immediate ancestors were born, grew up, and died under the umbrella and central figure of the modern State. Our minds have been molded by submission and obedience to a central and hierarchical power.

We have to go back to the seventeenth century to find the ideological origin of the modern State and the justification of its power with the concept of sovereignty.[3] This concept, which is so easy for us to understand, is now going through a sudden stage of aging. Today, we are witnessing the growth of a new decentralized sovereignty called the Internet.

State power has reached its peak in our time. Some have called it a monopoly of violence.[4] But that power is losing its vigor. The reason is simple. The centralized, hierarchical model of government is diametrically opposed to the Internet. Unlike the State, the Internet is a global, decentralized computer network that allows people all over the world to be directly connected, without violence.

The organization of the State is generally divided into three branches: executive, legislative, and judicial. Citizens are subject to the rules of these powers, not by choice, but by national or local imposition. In addition, States maintain peer-to-peer relationships with other States, that is, peer-to-peer (P2P) in the strict sense. These relationships are precisely the key to the Internet. On a basic level, hierarchy no longer prevails, but equality.

---

[3] The Peace of Westphalia in 1648 put an end to the Thirty Years' War. After centuries of wars in Europe, the idea of sovereignty emerged as a means of defense and organization to prevent bloody border encroachments.

[4] The phrase "monopoly of violence" is widely attributed to the German sociologist and philosopher Max Weber. In his seminal work Politics as a Vocation (1919), Weber defines the modern State in terms of its legitimate monopoly on the use of physical force. Many libertarians also use this expression to advocate a State whose power is reduced to fulfill its essential functions: protecting private property, life, and the free market. This idea can be realized thanks to the Internet Revolution.

This does not happen because of ideology, but because of technology.[5] Since its creation, people all over the world have been able to maintain peer-to-peer relationships without the need for a central entity. This represents a Copernican turn in the way we understand the world.

The most famous phrase of the 1960s was the one uttered by astronaut Neil Armstrong upon stepping on the moon in July 1969, when he said: "One small step for man, one giant leap for mankind."[6] The myopic world looked at the moon.

However, in the bowels of the U.S. Pentagon, the real big step for mankind was being prepared: the conception of the world's first decentralized network, ARPANET, later baptized "the Internet."

This digital embryo grew in computer connections, nodes, and networks until it became a bouncy baby. Its first serious game was a rattle of spam messages in the 1970s.[7] In the 1990s, it put on the bib of the World Wide Web (www) and began to slurp away nonstop. Businesses had no choice but to adapt to the little

---

[5] Many libertarians defend theories of reducing State power. But this step will not be brought about by ideology, but by technology. Once the Internet offers more practical and effective solutions to people's problems, the State will have no choice but to improve, reduce its structure, and devote itself to serving its citizens. The State will not change because of nice ideas, but because it will have no choice. First comes technology, then ideology.

[6] NASA.gov, August 28, 2012, "Who Was Neil Armstrong? (Grades 5–8)" Accessed on July 29, 2024.

[7] The first spam email was discovered on May 3, 1978, by Gary Thuerk.

tyrant by advertising and creating pages on that “www” site that gradually grew bigger.

Numerous websites were created, which meant a good binge for the little fellow, who in the end had no choice but to throw up most of them. It was the dot-com bubble.

The next succulent dish for the Internet was telematic communication, which we commonly call email. Here, the Internet put on its boots without hesitation. It had no interest in postal letters or faxes, which seemed to be inventions of a prehistoric past.

At present, nearly 300 billion emails are sent every day, not an inconsiderable figure.[8] The Internet tends to correct obsessive behavior, which is why a system was invented to avoid spam messages in 1997. It is the system called Proof of Work, used in Bitcoin and attributed to Adam Back.

The adolescence of the Internet was typical of anyone: it started snooping. Hence, the emergence of the Google search engine in 1997. It also tried to listen to pirated music with Napster in 1999, but was banned. It tried to socialize in a decentralized way with social networks, and Facebook emerged in 2004. In 2005, it started watching videos on YouTube. In 2006, it was allowed to use music legally with Spotify.

In 2007, the Internet decided to have a more personal connection system with the iPhone. It also

---

[8] The World: A Brief Introduction. Richard Haass. (Chapter, “The Internet, Cyberspace and Cybersecurity.” Penguin Press.)

started going to the movies with the emergence of Netflix. After the success of smartphones, the Internet entered its adult and professional age. First, it changed the banking business with fintech.[9] But it did not stop there. Its ambition has no limits.

The Internet also wanted to issue its own money without depending on anyone, neither States, nor governments, nor trusted third parties. That is why in 2009, it created Bitcoin, its first native currency. In 2015, a system for creating decentralized platforms appeared through smart contracts: Ethereum. The Internet has also found a traveling companion: Artificial Intelligence. Between the two, they have set out to change the world.

In the 1990s, legal scholars pointed out "code is law," that is, the code contained in software is Law. But for the Internet, this is insufficient. It wants a new law emanating from a jurisdiction of its own, the Internet Jurisdiction.

This is based on its decentralized nature. It is a virtual law, self-executing, and based on the sovereignty of the community. Of course, it is issued

---

[9] Fintech companies are businesses that use technology to offer financial services. The term "fintech" comes from combining the words financial and technology. These companies often leverage artificial intelligence, big data, blockchain, and cloud computing to improve and transform various aspects of the financial sector. Examples include mobile payments, peer-to-peer lending, crowdfunding, investment management, insurance, and cryptocurrencies. Fintech has gained popularity by providing more accessible, faster, and more personalized financial solutions than many traditional institutions.

without the need for States, governments, or trusted third parties.

Law as we know it today is changing. We are witnessing one of the biggest legal changes in history. This new law is called Digital Law, or Law 3.0, and it unfolds its effects in a new Jurisdiction, that of the Internet.

I. Digital Laws, Bitcoin, and Internet Jurisdiction

"We need new laws. Laws fitting the times we live in, with the world that surrounds us. Not laws built on the basis of the past. Laws built for today, laws that will fit tomorrow".

(Cyberpunk Manifesto). Christian As. Kirtchev, 1997.

1. The Birth of Internet Jurisdiction

On January 3, 2009, someone under the pseudonym Satoshi Nakamoto created the first block of the Bitcoin blockchain, called the genesis block. The second block was generated exactly six days later.[10] This coincides with the six days it took God to create the world, according to the account in Genesis, the first book of the Bible.

Satoshi is not one of those people who leave things to chance. This coincidence was a nod to the new world that was being born, the new Internet Jurisdiction.

Nakamoto's proposal was ambitious but not difficult to grasp: to digitally regulate a new payment system. In more technical terms, it would be a system of electronic cash that does not pass through a financial institution. This is what can be gleaned from his founding document, called a whitepaper, titled Bitcoin: A Peer to Peer Electronic Cash System.[11]

Inventing a new digital payment system would already have been remarkable, but the mysterious figure actually created something much more relevant. It was nothing more and nothing less than a new digital regulatory system, an alternative to the State and

---

[10] George B. (January 5, 2023). "The Genesis Block: The First Bitcoin Block." Coindesk. Accessed October 2, 2024.

[11] Nakamoto, S. (2008). Bitcoin: A Peer-to-Peer Electronic Cash System.

operating in the Internet Jurisdiction. Bitcoin is not merely a digital currency. It is a Digital Law. Specifically, it is the first Digital Law of many that have followed.

Bitcoin was born outside any traditional system. It was not approved by any State or public body. It was not submitted to the World Bank or the International Monetary Fund. No parliament voted for or against its implementation. It was simply deployed in an atypical, digital jurisdiction with its own rules, called the Internet Jurisdiction.

Traditional State rules are issued by public bodies and deploy their effects within one territory. They can also operate in several countries at the same time by virtue of international agreements between States. A clear example is the international treaties of the European Union, which produce effects in several countries.

Digital Laws such as Bitcoin unfold their effects in a first layer called the Internet Jurisdiction and operate under the technical principle of decentralization. In this Jurisdiction, the effects are produced independently of the States.

For example, if a user, Alice, sends a small amount of Bitcoin, something like 0.0001 BTC,[12] from her wallet, cryptoasset wallet to Bob's wallet, that payment will be sealed in a block and cannot be changed. The

[12] Bitcoin cents are called satoshis, so in the example, it would be 10,000 satoshis.

effects on this first layer will happen. No matter how many weapons they have, how much media they manipulate, or how many Bitcoins they own, States, the powers that be, or Bill Gates will not be able to change the transaction. For some, this fact may seem irrelevant, but it really represents a before and after in the way we operate and, for the purposes of this book, in the way we legislate.

Bitcoin is like Christopher Columbus. When it was born under the umbrella of the States, we all thought that jurisdiction was flat and centralized. Now it turns out that there is also a jurisdiction that is round and decentralized.

That is what is difficult for someone molded to the patterns of the modern world to understand. Moreover, this Internet Jurisdiction is so strong that it is practically unbreakable. It is stronger than all the constitutions of all countries put together. The bottom line is that with Bitcoin, a simple digital currency was not, but an entire new Internet Jurisdiction was born.

Seen from this point of view, Bitcoin does have value. As I will explain, the Internet Jurisdiction obeys technical principles that are diametrically opposed to those of the States. This has very relevant practical consequences.

For example, on the Internet, anyone can issue Digital Laws without belonging to a political party, government, or State. In legal, political, and economic terms, Bitcoin is a wild revolution.

From the point of view of the Internet Jurisdiction, States operate in a second layer. Specifically, it is in this second layer that States may or may not recognize the legal effects of what happens in the first layer, the Internet Jurisdiction. There is a fundamental principle of law that governs this second layer: each State can do whatever it wants in its own territory, unless it is invaded or suffers other illegitimate interference, in which case it will be another State or a factual power that decides.

One jurisdiction in this second layer that does not recognize what happens on the Internet, the first layer, as having legal effect on its territory is China. The 0.0001 BTC transaction mentioned above is sealed and immovable in the Internet Jurisdiction.

China has expressly prohibited the effects of that transaction on its territory, but in fact, the transaction has already occurred and produced effects on layer one. For Bob, therefore, the solution is simple. He will have to go to another jurisdiction in the second layer to apply earthly legal effects to his transaction. At this moment, he has many destinations to choose from.

This brings us to another consequence. Bob will be able to choose a State that treats him well fiscally. Imagine that instead of 0.0001 BTC, Bob receives several million dollars in Bitcoin for services rendered or for the sale of a good, all perfectly legal.

Normally, he will choose a jurisdiction where he has legal certainty on the one hand and pays less tax on the other. The State then ceases to be central and becomes a service provider. In this way, States will have to compete to attract clients, regardless of their nationality.

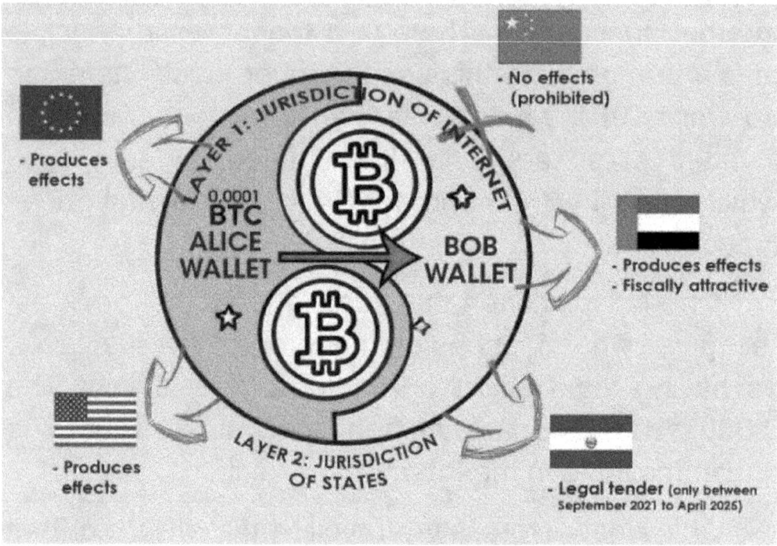

Fig. 1. The Internet Jurisdiction layer and the State Jurisdiction layer.

From the above, we can conclude several things. First, the possibility of issuing digital laws is open to anyone without any need for State backing. In other words, anyone can create their own cryptoasset, provided there is a serious project behind it. Every cryptoasset that has real value is a Digital Law. The ability to create Digital Laws no longer belongs only to States, but to anyone. This opens up opportunities that were unthinkable for those of us born under the boot of the State.

Second, the Internet Jurisdiction, layer one, operates and produces effects independently of what happens in the Jurisdiction of States, layer two. Bitcoin is the best example. No one can stop it. Some have imagined a world in which all States agree to ban cryptoassets such as Bitcoin.

The truth is that the world's States have never been able to agree on anything, not even on how to tackle climate change. It seems more likely that rulers will wipe out the world with atomic bombs than that they will unanimously decide to ban Bitcoin.

On the other hand, many States have a vested interest in seeing Bitcoin and cryptocurrencies flourish. Likewise, when starting a project that will affect a blockchain, it will become increasingly important to choose the client State from which you operate. It is the upside-down world of the modern State.

Third, the State is ceasing to be the center of power. History repeats itself over and over again. In the seventeenth century, there was a very relevant figure around whom everything revolved, King Louis XIV of France, known as the Sun King. He was a figure who humbly stated that "the State is me." Power chooses the hands in which it wants to rest. And it seems to be abandoning the State and moving toward the Internet.

2. Bitcoin, the First Digital Law

Until the birth of Bitcoin, it was unthinkable that the issuance of a currency could thrive without the solidity of traditional regulation, outside the financial system, and without the presence of States or official institutions. This is precisely one of the main reasons why many believe that Bitcoin is not real, is worthless, and is a mere ethereal invention.

The reality is that Bitcoin and crypto assets continue to grow steadily. Many gurus have predicted their apocalyptic end, but it never comes[13]. Every new obituary is quickly contradicted by fresh data on adoption, liquidity, and network security, which shows that what many dismissed as a fad has behaved more like a robust, evolving protocol than a speculative mirage.

Both the number of global users and the value of the digital currency continue to grow. In 2023, 420 million Bitcoin holders were counted worldwide[14]. To give you an idea, there are already more Bitcoin

---

[13] The website https://99bitcoins.com/bitcoin-obituaries/%20 highlights the number of times that various people have prophesied the end of Bitcoin. At the time of writing, there are 474 announcements of Bitcoin's death in October 2023.

[14] There are several media that provide this data. It is not about quoting countless sources, so I refer this publication: Criptonoticias (January 19, 2023). "Número de usuarios de Bitcóin y criptomonedas creció 40% en 2022: reporte." Accessed October 2, 2024 from https://www.criptonoticias.com/comunidad/adopcion/numero-usuarios-bitcoin-criptomonedas-crecio-40-2022-reporte/

holders than users of the social network X (Twitter)[15]. In practical terms, this means that Bitcoin is no longer a niche tool for specialists but a monetary technology that millions of ordinary people, companies, and even institutions are learning to hold, move, and integrate into their daily lives.

Bitcoin is the first Digital Law operating in the Internet Jurisdiction. One of the most repeated criticisms against the crypto asset is that it is not regulated. Every now and then, the official school of thought reminds us of this. If a catastrophic event occurs in the crypto world, Central Bank authorities come back to the lack of regulation. However, State regulation is not a guarantee of absolute safety and compliance either.

I agree that State regulation (layer two) of Digital Laws born in Internet Jurisdiction (layer one) will help the community grow and mature. The latter is essential in any social, cultural, and political change. But the criticism of the lack of regulation (by States) ignores another reality, which I consider to be the true virtue of Bitcoin.

Bitcoin is itself law. Bitcoin is itself regulated by digital law. Its rulebook is written directly in open source code, enforced by thousands of independent nodes instead of by police, courts, or ministries.

---

[15] Fernandez, R. (March 4, 2024). X (Twitter) – Statistical data. Statista. Accessed on October 2, 2024, from https://es.statista.com/temas/10170/twitter-datos-mundiales/#topicOverview

The guarantees come from mathematics and consensus, not from decrees or bureaucratic promises. Of course, critics of the mainstream view omit this fact, either out of ignorance or out of self-interested manipulation.

Bitcoin is a digital currency that works properly. It has no structural flaws at the protocol level that would prevent it from doing what it promises to do: settle transactions securely and predictably. It can be categorically stated that Bitcoin is very well regulated, or that it is very well regulated. By studying this new law, we can conclude that, from a practical point of view, Bitcoin is a better law than traditional law in many specific aspects of monetary issuance, scarcity, and settlement.

The big question then is what kind of regulation Bitcoin represents. What kind of law is Bitcoin? What is the legal nature of this new law? Bitcoin and the other cryptocurrencies, at least those that provide value, are a new form of regulation that emanates from and produces its effects on and for the Internet.

With the birth of the Internet and the proliferation of software in the 1990s, the theory that "Code is Law"[16] was developed. But Bitcoin goes one step further. In

---

[16] Lawrence Lessig, in his book Code and Other Laws of Cyberspace (1999), argued that computer code (the software and protocols that structure the Internet) acts as a form of regulation, similar to traditional laws. For him, the rules implemented in software are regulations. For example, who can access certain data, how online transactions are handled, and what types of behavior are allowed on a digital platform. In short, through code, user behavior can be regulated.

addition to code, it has blockchain technology. Therefore, the Bitcoin source code becomes a non-derogable law[17]. Only with rigorous mechanisms can these standards be modified.

Unlike a statute that can be rewritten overnight by a parliamentary majority, any serious change to Bitcoin requires broad technical consensus, public review, and, ultimately, the voluntary adoption of the new version by thousands of participants. I elaborate more on these issues in chapter three. In summary, I write that Bitcoin and cryptocurrencies are virtual (digital), private law (emanating from the community itself, not from the States)[18].

Likewise, we find ourselves with a law that is executive: it deploys its effects through a decentralized peer-to-peer network, with self-executing mechanisms (using smart contracts). These are neither contracts nor smart, but software code that is automatically executed when certain predefined conditions are met.

We are contemplating the dawn of a new law emanating directly from the Internet. It is the law native to the Internet, also called digital law or Law 3.0. For the first time, large-scale legal and economic behavior

---

[17] Undoubtedly, Bitcoin has the characteristics of code described by Lessig, that is, with a source code, software, and algorithms to regulate a currency operating in a digital space. The blockchain is a ledger of transactions contained in a distributed manner that cannot be deleted, erased, or manipulated. This strength makes Bitcoin not mere code, but digital law, that is, law.

[18] Bitcoin is regulated through an open source protocol, which is maintained and updated by a community of voluntarily cooperating developers from all over the world. This protocol establishes the essential rules of Bitcoin, called "Bitcoin Core". Access the Bitcoin source code here: https://github.com/bitcoin/bitcoin

can be coordinated globally through software rules that do not care about borders, office hours, or political cycles.

Claiming that Bitcoin is unregulated is akin to a Martian, assuming they exist, criticizing the dollar because it is unregulated on their planet. Of course, the dollar or the euro is not regulated on Mars, simply because they belong to a different jurisdiction on a different planet in the solar system. When mainstream pundits keep repeating that Bitcoin is unregulated, they are really reminding us that Bitcoin belongs to another jurisdiction.

However, the criticism of the non-regulation of Bitcoin and crypto assets is evidence of three things.

Firstly, we are witnessing an emerging and therefore unknown market. Not everyone can understand the birth of a new legal system of Digital Law operating in the Internet Jurisdiction. It is therefore understandable that some do not fully understand what Bitcoin and cryptocurrencies have to offer.

This confusion is heightened by volatility, media noise, and scams that parasitize every technological revolution, which often leads observers to judge the entire ecosystem by its worst actors rather than by its most serious innovations.

Secondly, these critics should be reminded of Michael Kremer's argument[19]. He argues that the fundamental driver of human progress is not commodities, but technological solutions to problems.

It is very curious that the same people who criticize and hinder technological developments insist that the solution for human survival lies in raw materials. Once they have convinced us of this, they warn that the world is at great risk of losing its only salvation, raw materials. That is why they impose tight controls on their use, production, or sale.

As Julian L. Simon argued in his book The Last Resort, natural resources and energy are becoming less scarce, the world's food supply is improving, and population growth is advantageous in the long run, while pollution is decreasing. In short, to quote J. L. Simon himself: "Human beings are not just mouths to feed, but productive and inventive minds that help find creative solutions to man's problems, thus leaving us better off over the long run"[20].

The fact is that mankind's greatest asset is precisely man himself. Digital Law fits squarely within this vision: it is a technological response to the problem of how to coordinate economic life without handing absolute power to centralized intermediaries.

---

[19] Kremer, M. (1993). Population growth and technological change: One million B.C. to 1990. The Quarterly Journal of Economics, 108(3), 681–716.

[20] Moore, S. (s.f.). "Un homenaje a Julian Simon." Liberalismo.org. Accessed October 2, 2024, from https://www.liberalismo.org/articulo/185/82/homenaje/julian/simon/

Hence, the technological relevance of Bitcoin, Ethereum, and the rest of the Digital Laws that are emerging in the Internet Jurisdiction. Until the birth of Bitcoin, technology had not made it possible for digital laws to be issued in a decentralized manner by the community. Moreover, technology has another great advantage, and that is that it is an unrivalled asset.

A person who benefits from an invention does not reduce the utility it gives to others who use it[21]. No matter how much Bitcoin is mined, transmitted, or possessed, it does not cease to have value. No matter how many millions of times a Bitcoin is sent from one wallet to another, it will not wear out.

Ethereum was also another technological revolution. The second most important digital law after Bitcoin, it allows the private issuance of digital standards of various kinds. In other words, anyone can issue their own crypto asset. This is why, since Ethereum, it is possible to digitally represent rights and obligations in a token[22], which is known as tokenizing.

The traditional common system of this new digital mechanism is the bearer note[23]. With Ethereum, the

---

[21] Ammous, S. (2018). The Bitcoin Standard. Deusto.

[22] Bitcoin allows making payments and not issuing new tokens like Ethereum. The community is looking for solutions such as the Lightning Network, which is second-layer solution built on top of the Bitcoin blockchain to give more agility. In addition to the RGB protocol, designed to enable the construction of Turing-complete, scalable, and confidential smart contracts over the Bitcoin network and Lightning Network.

[23] It is a financial instrument that is not assigned to a specific beneficiary. The physical holder of the note has the right to claim what the note represents, either

bearer note is a token, or digital asset. A company share, a concert ticket, a right to future income, or a participation in a project can all be encoded as tokens, making them easier to divide, transfer, and audit in real time across the globe.

Finally, and thirdly, the regulation of States in the long term will help to have a more mature community. It is true that some will refuse to enter this new market. But for the new generations, buying bread or coffee with crypto assets will not be rare.

They will not invest in shares, but in tokens. For them, it will not be a risky opportunity, but a way of life, like going to the cinema or playing sports. In that context, clear but reasonable State rules can act as guardrails that filter out fraud without suffocating the creativity of open source communities.

State regulation will help the mass acceptance of crypto assets. However, Bitcoin, Ethereum, and other crypto assets have taught us that the real regulation of Internet Jurisdiction does not belong to the States, but to the community itself.

---

a sum of money or an asset. Bearer notes are anonymous, since payment is made to whoever holds the note at the time of presentation, without the need to identify prior ownership or title. This type of instrument includes certain types of checks, bonds, and, most commonly, bank bills.

3. The Market of Digital Laws and Community Sovereignty

Each digital law deploys its effects in a decentralized, non-hierarchical manner. It is the community that freely chooses to submit to digital regulation. As each blockchain requires a crypto asset to operate, the community must acquire that crypto asset. In other words, every major Digital Law has both a legal dimension, in the form of rules encoded in software, and an economic dimension, in the form of a token that users must hold to participate in that rule system.

When Bitcoin began to operate, Satoshi Nakamoto, in addition to publishing his whitepaper and deploying the protocol, sought a community that would begin to test his invention. A very interesting and recommendable free book about how Satoshi Nakamoto tried to generate a community is The Book of Satoshi[24].

It collects all the emails that Satoshi wrote to different people in relation to Bitcoin. Those early exchanges on cryptography mailing lists, forums, and code repositories show how a handful of curious developers slowly turned a theoretical paper into a living, breathing monetary network.

---

[24] You can download this book for free: https://libroblockchain.com/satoshi/ (Spanish version)

Satoshi got more and more users to study and test Bitcoin. Little by little, the number of Bitcoin holders and miners increased. Bitcoin, like any crypto asset, is worthless without a community. It is like a king without a kingdom, or a State without a people.

The same process occurred with Ethereum, which has one of the most active communities in the crypto asset market. Developers, entrepreneurs, artists, and activists use Ethereum daily to experiment with new economic models, governance systems, and digital goods, reinforcing the idea that a Digital Law lives or dies by the strength of its community.

For the Digital Laws of the Internet, the concept of community is very relevant. Community replaces the idea of people in Rousseau's conception of the social contract. In the jurisdiction of the Internet, sovereignty is not local; it is universal.

And it is not vested in national citizens, but in anyone with access to the Internet. Sovereignty is no longer of the people, but of the community. The community is not united through a State but through the Internet. It is therefore made up of users from all over the world, an approach that generates notable differences with traditional legal systems.

The first is that in traditional law, laws are made by a group, the government, which has usually been democratically elected. In contrast, in Internet Jurisdiction, anyone can issue Digital Laws. This leads us to another consequence: the best Digital Laws, in general, are those that are accepted by the community in the long term, because they have value.

A token that no one wants to hold or use, no matter how ambitious its whitepaper, will not survive, while a modest but useful protocol with a committed community can endure for years.

The second is that there is freedom to submit to a rule, regardless of place or nationality. The new way of issuing Digital Laws is based on a decentralized democracy. There are currently more than 2.5 million Digital Laws in force[25]. This number is increasing with each passing day. Many of these laws lack value or sovereignty, because they are hardly used by the community. Others, on the contrary, are very useful and valued.

Digital Laws are deployed not in a State or country, but in a digital market that operates on the Internet. Digital Laws are legal products that users choose to consume for their own purposes. A person may interact with one Digital Law to save, another to borrow, another to play, and another to prove identity, all without ever crossing a physical border.

Here we come to the third difference. The freedom of choice of Digital Laws by the community generates greater legislative competition. Since there is no hierarchical imposition, submission is voluntary to what

---

[25] Daly, L. (August 19, 2024). "How many cryptocurrencies are there?" The Motley Fool. Accessed October 2, 2024, from https://www.fool.com/investing/stock-market/market-sectors/financials/cryptocurrency-stocks/how-many-cryptocurrencies-are-there/

is considered the best norm. This is why Gresham's Law is applied to Digital Laws. This economic principle holds that, in a system of money circulation with currencies of different values, overvalued currency will tend to be withdrawn from circulation and hoarded, while undervalued currency will be used for everyday transactions[26].

The essence of Gresham's Law can be summarized in a popular phrase: "Bad money drives out good money." This means that when people have the option of using two currencies of different values, they will tend to retain and use the currency they consider more valuable or of higher intrinsic value, while spending or circulating the currency they consider less valuable.

The higher appreciation of a Digital Law is not only speculative, but it is also related to the content or proposal of the Digital Law, that is, its intrinsic value. In the crypto world, this can be seen when users choose to hold scarce assets like Bitcoin for the long term while using more inflationary or utility-focused tokens for daily operations and experimentation.

A good Digital Law will have sovereignty, because it will attract the community. A bad Digital Law will be like a summer storm. It will attract speculators, the price

---

[26] This principle was named after Sir Thomas Gresham, a 16th-century English financier who observed it in practice during his time as financial advisor to the British Crown.

of the crypto asset will rise, and soon it will fall and remain in a state of latent mortality.

Some will think that Gresham's Law applies to crypto assets because they are simply currencies, but not Digital Laws. This is a mistake. To say that Bitcoin is not regulated, I insist, is the same as saying that the dollar or the euro is not regulated. They are, but they belong to different jurisdictions.

The fourth difference is that in this Digital Law market, you can get objective data that helps to understand the importance that a regulation has in the community. All Digital Laws issue a crypto asset. For example, the two most important Digital Laws, Bitcoin and Ethereum, have issued Bitcoin (BTC) and Ether (ETH) as their native crypto assets.

The more a Digital Law is used, the more users in the community will acquire its crypto asset [27]. Therefore, Digital Laws, unlike what happens with the rules issued by the State[28], have an objective scale of valuation in which there is no room for direct manipulation by the State. The Austrian school of economics advocates a free market without State intervention.

---

[27] There is also a subjective factor that can be added, and that is the speculation that takes place.

[28] Despite this, manipulation by the issuers of the Digital Laws themselves is often observed. All that glitters is not gold.

This principle is de facto applicable to the Digital Law market[29]. Prices are discovered continuously in open markets, where anyone with an Internet connection can observe and verify them in real time.

#	Name		Price	1h %	24h %	7d %	▾ Market Cap	Volume(24h)
1	Bitcoin BTC	Buy	$93,016.41	▴0.66%	▴1.67%	▴3.52%	$1,856,343,055,343	$79,467,054,489 855.09K
2	Ethereum ETH	Buy	$3,130.78	▴1.25%	▴3.73%	▴3.41%	$377,871,180,399	$27,110,381,577 8.66M
3	Tether USDT	Buy	$1.00	▴0.01%	▾0.02%	▴0.04%	$184,739,531,801	$117,494,195,255 117.45B
4	XRP XRP	Buy	$2.18	▴0.64%	▴0.58%	▾2.23%	$131,890,737,200	$4,134,174,214 1.89B
5	BNB BNB	Buy	$907.42	▴0.77%	▴3.43%	▴2.27%	$124,984,635,927	$2,737,697,120 3.01M
6	Solana SOL	Buy	$142.02	▴0.76%	▴1.79%	▴0.89%	$79,501,441,822	$5,534,393,822 39.10M
7	USDC USDC	Buy	$0.9999	▴0.01%	▾0.03%	▴0.01%	$77,768,732,160	$13,931,754,784 13.93B
8	TRON TRX	Buy	$0.2789	▴0.03%	▾1.25%	▴1.24%	$26,411,157,115	$601,117,631 2.15B
9	Dogecoin DOGE	Buy	$0.1515	▴0.97%	▴3.49%	▾2.64%	$24,488,186,024	$1,508,424,615 9.95B
10	Cardano ADA	Buy	$0.4434	▴1.36%	▴3.07%	▴2.98%	$15,919,880,004	$854,087,288 1.92B
11	Bitcoin Cash BCH	Buy	$596.15	▾0.57%	▴8.84%	▴9.19%	$11,900,266,751	$791,386,518 1.32M

Fig. 2: Leading Digital Laws by market capitalization.

With the data provided by the market cap[30] of crypto assets, we can know the distribution of sovereignty of the Digital Laws. Bitcoin is the sovereign currency par excellence with half of the jurisdiction of

[29] The Austrian School argues that the State distorts prices, altering the crucial signals for the efficient allocation of resources in an economy. According to this view, prices emerge from voluntary interactions between buyers and sellers and reflect subjective information about the value of goods and services. State interference, whether through price controls, manipulation of the money supply, or excessive regulation, is seen as leading to market imbalances, waste of resources, and loss of economic efficiency. The greatest manipulation of information also occurs when a State changes the value of its currency, since it will affect the rest of the market. It would be like altering the blood, since it will affect the rest of the body's organs. With cryptocurrencies and decentralization, these kinds of manipulations are more difficult, or at least they follow other rules.

[30] Market cap, or market capitalization, refers to the total market value of a blockchain's outstanding crypto assets.

the Internet[31]. Ethereum is the second, with about 20 percent of the market.

At the time of writing, these are the top Digital Laws by market capitalization[32].

The fifth difference is that Digital Laws are under constant scrutiny by the community, who test their validity for errors or flaws. For this reason, some Digital Laws are overturned swiftly, in as little as twenty-four hours.

This was the case of the stable currency Terra/Luna, which, in May 2022, and being one of the ten most important currencies in the market, was devalued by 99 percent in a matter of hours. Terra USD was a stable currency that had the dollar as its reference value.

Instead of using dollars, fiat money, as collateral, it used another cryptocurrency, Luna, whose issuance varied to make each Terra token worth one dollar. Through an algorithm, users were incentivized to burn, that is, destroy, Luna or Terra (UST) to achieve parity with the dollar.

Employing a graphical example, Terra/Luna worked like a seesaw in a playground. The two crypto assets would rise or fall to try to achieve parity with the dollar. Depending on the price of Terra USD, more of one cryptocurrency or the other was sold to reach a

---

[31] This data varies, but is approximate.

[32] https://coinmarketcap.com

one-dollar value. The attack on the algorithm sought to generate such inflation in the Luna coin that it, in turn, plummeted the value of the Terra coin (UST). They broke the balance of the seesaw by putting too much weight on one end and then pulling back suddenly.

The last few who sat on the seesaw are still feeling the pain in their behinds, and in their wallets. The graph in Figure 3 summarizes the events that occurred.

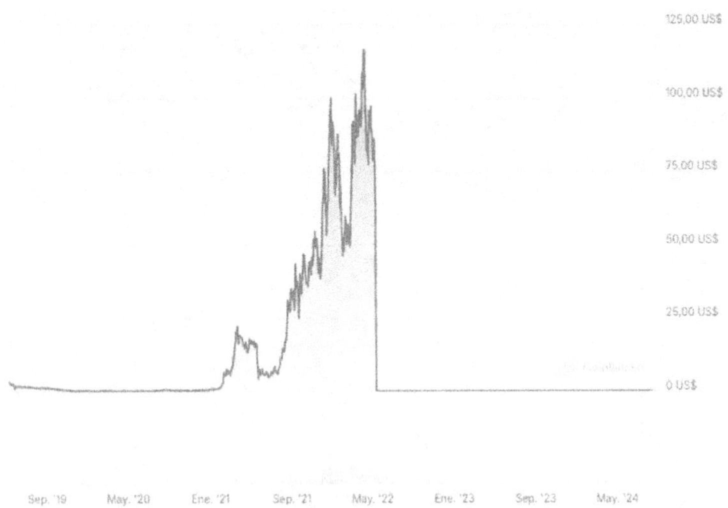

Fig. 3: Source: coingecko.com

The Terra/Luna collapse is a powerful reminder that not all Digital Laws are created equal: elegant code is not enough if the underlying economic design can be pushed into a death spiral by a coordinated attack or by market panic.

Finally, Digital Laws are public, and anyone can copy and modify their code by issuing a new Digital

Law. Technology is, by its nature, a non-excludable good.

This is a great advantage since once one person invents something; everyone else can copy it and benefit from it[33]. In this sense, the Digital Law ecosystem behaves like an open scientific field, where ideas are forked, improved, and recombined, and where innovation accelerates precisely because no single actor can lock the rules away behind closed doors.

---

[33] Ammous, S. (2018). "The Bitcoin standard". Deusto.

4. First Digital Laws Issued in the Internet Jurisdiction

I will briefly introduce some of the first Digital Laws issued by the Internet Jurisdiction. These early projects work like case studies, showing how the community has experimented in public with new legal ideas and technical architecture that try to improve what already existed. While there are projects that do not contribute to anything, there are others that do.

It is important to understand that the Internet Jurisdiction continues to grow and mature. Most of the Digital Laws we will review did not come from parliaments or ministries, but from groups of developers and users who organized themselves online without asking the States for permission.

I recognize that reading legal norms, both traditional and digital, can feel like an act of heroism and effort. This is normal. Not everyone is prepared to study law, and Digital Laws are real law. That is why I have decided to provide more information through footnotes, to which I refer.

If at any point you feel overwhelmed by names or technicalities, you can always jump ahead and focus on a small group of key Digital Laws: Bitcoin, Ethereum, and Tether, which together offer a clear overview of the terrain.

4.1. Bitcoin (BTC) Digital Law.

Bitcoin is the first Digital Law in history. It was issued on January 3, 2009, and many in the community celebrate its birthday every year on that date. Although Bitcoin may seem complex at first glance, its legislative proposal is very simple: to regulate a deflationary digital currency. In practice, this means a currency with a limited supply that is designed to protect its purchasing power over time instead of constantly losing it.

Why and under what conditions this can happen is explained throughout the book. It is perhaps the most important feature of this virtual currency. The central question is to understand why, over the long term, it is expected to rise in value.

Bitcoin deliberately targeted a market niche that seemed almost impossible to reach: competing with the currencies issued by the United States, known as legal tender or fiat money. What happens with these currencies is that they are inflationary[34], that is, they lose value. Historically, many of them have eventually been worth close to zero.

The money with which you are paid, the money you keep in your checking account or in your pocket, is worth a little less every day. In some countries, this erosion is slow and almost invisible, and in others, it is

[34] Some proponents of this fiat money issuance system claim that inflation is controlled. Be that as it may, they are inflationary currencies, unlike Bitcoin.

brutal, wiping out savings and salaries in a few months and generating enormous poverty.

Bitcoin has been able to compete with these currencies for technical reasons. As David was able to defeat Goliath with a slingshot, the small Bitcoin, with blockchain technology, is fighting against the currencies of the strongest.

There is a very important date to recall whenever we talk about fiat money: August 15, 1971. On that day, the President of the United States, Richard Nixon, decreed that the dollar would no longer be backed by gold.

In other words, from that date onward, the United States could issue dollars without being tied to a fixed quantity of gold. This has been described by some as non-stop printing or flooding the world with banknotes. It was the end of the gold standard. Since that date, inflation, that is, the loss of value of money, has grown exponentially.

At the moment, the public debt of the United States is around 35 trillion dollars. This is not only a staggering figure in absolute terms, but it is also a reminder of how dependent the current monetary system is on the constant creation of new debt and new units of currency.

Against this backdrop, the Bitcoin proposal becomes clearer. It is to issue a deflationary digital currency, a good currency according to Gresham's Law, which does not exist in the jurisdiction of the United States after the end of the gold standard.

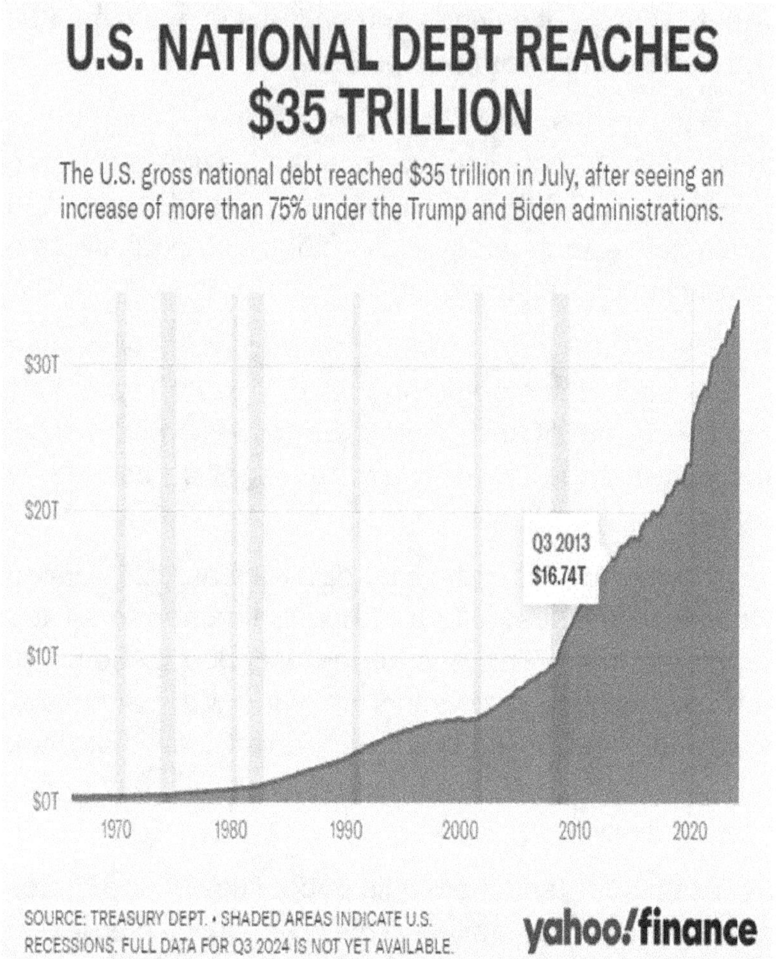

Fig. 4.

The code that regulates Bitcoin can only be modified if very specific conditions are met. These rules are therefore predefined, and using Bitcoin necessarily implies accepting them. It is a take it or leave it system with no hotline to call for exceptions or special favors.

On the virtues of Bitcoin, I recommend reading chapter 9, "What Bitcoin Is Good For, in Saifedean Ammous' book The Bitcoin Standard. As I said, Bitcoin is the most valuable crypto asset, with a dominance of about fifty percent of the market.

More about this Digital Law can be found in Chapter 3.

4.2. Namecoin Digital Law (NMC).

Issued in April 2011, this Digital Law proposed the creation of decentralized Internet domains, an alternative to the current system of .com, .org, and similar suffixes, using the .bit extension[35].

Two things are especially interesting about this legislative proposal. First, Namecoin was one of the earliest cryptocurrencies to explore alternative uses of blockchain technology beyond simply being a means of value exchange, in this case, using it as a registry for names and identifiers.

The second is that it uses the same code base as Bitcoin. It only makes a few specific modifications to allow decentralized registration of domain names and other data on its blockchain[36].

---

[35] For example, .bit domain names are stored on the Namecoin blockchain, which provides them with a high level of security and resistance to censorship. In addition to domain names, Namecoin can also be used to register and transfer other types of data, such as identities and public keys.

[36] Although Namecoin and Bitcoin share a common history and the same code base, they are independent projects with different goals and functionalities. As I noted earlier, Digital Laws are generally open source and can be copied by anyone.

This legislative proposal ultimately did not have much traction with the community. Using Internet domains in a decentralized manner is, at this time, not something very attractive to the community.

That could change in the future if censorship or centralized control over domain names becomes a more visible problem and tools like Namecoin reappear as part of the solution.

4.3. Litecoin Digital Law (LTC).

This Digital Law was issued in October 2011. Its legislative proposal was to regulate an alternative currency compatible with Bitcoin. Just as Bitcoin is considered digital gold, Litecoin was intended to be digital silver[37].

This Digital Law improved some technical aspects of Bitcoin. For example, it is faster and lighter, with a more accessible mining system[38]. Litecoin has a maximum supply of 84 million coins, four times more than the maximum supply of Bitcoin (21 million coins). This means that there will be more Litecoins in

---

[37] Haoyang Yu, Yutong Sun, Yulin Liu, and Luyao Zhang. In https://ideas.repec.org, "Bitcoin Gold, Litecoin Silver: An Introduction to Cryptocurrency's Valuation and Trading Strategy".

[38] The time to generate a block is shorter in Litecoin, approximately 2.5 minutes. Bitcoin has a block time of approximately 10 minutes. Litecoin's mining algorithm is different. While Bitcoin uses the SHA-256 algorithm, Litecoin uses Scrypt. This mining algorithm is more accessible to conventional hardware miners and allows for a wider distribution of hashing power in the network. In Bitcoin, there is a tendency for miners to join forces and reduce costs, which means that, paradoxically, there is a certain centralization of miners.

circulation compared to Bitcoin. Despite this, both are deflationary.

Litecoin has never been able to outperform Bitcoin. Even so, its long track record shows that there is room in the Internet Jurisdiction for secondary or complementary Digital Laws that learn from the pioneer but adjust parameters such as speed, supply, or mining in search of different trade-offs. It is interesting to note something mentioned before, namely that there is great competition among Digital Laws to improve those issued in the past.

That competition forces serious projects to constantly strive for excellence. Due to its proven technology and long history, Litecoin remains one of the most popular and widely accepted cryptocurrencies in the crypto market.

4.4. Peercoin Digital Law (PPC).

This Digital Law was issued in August 2012. Its proposal was to achieve greater energy efficiency by implementing an innovative consensus algorithm. As we well know from Bitcoin, there is no need for the intervention of a central entity. The simplest explanation I have found to explain consensus away from technicalities is that everything is replicated all at once through a technical mechanism. In this way, to attack the system, it must be done at the same time in all the copies deployed everywhere.

A consensus mechanism is used to carry out this copying from all to all. From a more technical point of view, it can be defined as the process by which network participants, or nodes, agree on the state of the network and the transactions to be added to the blockchain. This mechanism is essential to ensure that all copies of the blockchain distributed among the nodes remain synchronized and that the transactions recorded are valid.

In Bitcoin Digital Law, the consensus mechanism is Proof of Work30 [39] , which requires solving a mathematical equation. It demands higher energy consumption than other consensus mechanisms. Peercoin combines a mining or consensus system called Proof of Stake (PoS) with Proof of Work (PoW)[40].

Peercoin has no issuance limit, but it has controlled inflation. Each year, new Peercoin coins are generated at a rate of around 1 percent as a reward for block validators, both PoW and PoS. The project was an early attempt to answer a question that is now central in many debates: how to preserve decentralization and

---

[39] In my opinion, the best example of Proof of Work is the one that some websites force us to complete to confirm that we are human and not a mere bot. For example, pointing at traffic lights or moving arrows. In Bitcoin, the proof of work is done not by a physical person, but by a computer that has to solve mathematical equations. The more miners trying to solve the equation, the more complex it will be.

[40] In the PoW system, miners must solve computational problems to validate and secure transactions on the network, which is energy-intensive. In PoS, coin holders can participate in block validation and earn rewards based on how many coins they own and how long they keep them in their wallet. This helps reduce the energy consumption associated with cryptocurrency mining. Peercoin also seeks to strike a balance between security and decentralization by combining PoW and PoS. While PoW provides initial security and distributes coins more fairly in the initial phase of the network, PoS encourages long-term participation and reduces centralization by eliminating the need for expensive mining hardware.

security while reducing the environmental and economic cost of constantly burning energy.

4.5. Ripple (XRP) Digital Law.

This Digital Law was issued in 2012. Ripple regulates a payment platform and transaction settlement network through a company using its payment network, RippleNet, and its native cryptocurrency, XRP.

RippleNet sought a previously unexplored niche market: financial institutions and payment service providers. For this reason, this initiative was heavily criticized by part of the community. It was seen as selling out to the enemy. At its core, Ripple offers the advantages of blockchain technology, decentralized in origin, to centralized financial institutions, something that Bitcoin was precisely intended to avoid[41].

Many banks and financial institutions use this payment network, which is more agile, with centralized management by the company Ripple Labs. This company maintains significant control over the development, management, and governance of the network called RippleNet and its underlying technology.

[41] Ripple is not strictly speaking a blockchain, but rather a distributed ledger technology (DLT). The DLT concept is broader than blockchain. Not all DLTs are blockchains, but all blockchains are DLTs.

These are some of the entities that collaborate with Ripple: Banco Santander[42], BBVA[43], SBI Holdings[44], MUFG[45], and American Express[46], among others. Among the entities that have invested directly in Ripple, Standard Chartered Bank[47] stands out.

Just as other blockchains use Proof of Work (PoW) or Proof of Stake (PoS), the validation and confirmation of transactions in the RippleNet network is carried out by validators selected by Ripple Labs. This is typical of centralized entities.

Ripple Labs is also the main holder of the XRP cryptocurrency, with significant control over its

---

[42] Pirus, B. (July 9, 2020). Ripple partners with Santander for international payments. Cointelegraph. Accessed March 11, 2024, from https://es.cointelegraph.com/news/ripple-teams-up-with-santander-on-international-payments

[43] BBVA (May 17, 2018). "BBVA realiza transferencias internacionales en tiempo real entre Europa y México con Ripple". Accessed March 11, 2024, from https://www.bbva.com/es/bbva-realiza-transferencias-internacionales-tiempo-real-europa-mexico-ripple/

[44] Kapronasia (September 20, 2023). "SBI Holdings and Ripple step up their cooperation. Accessed March 11, 2024, from https://www.kapronasia.com/asia-payments-research-category/sbi-holdings-and-ripple-step-up-their-cooperation.html

[45] Suberg, W. (November 13, 2018). "Gigante bancario japonés MUFG firma memorando de entendimiento para desarrollar remesas basadas en Ripple a Brasil". Cointelegraph. Accessed March 11, 2024, from https://es.cointelegraph.com/news/japans-banking-giant-mufg-signs-mou-to-develop-ripple-based-remittances-to-brazil

[46] Peña, J. R. (November 16, 2017). "American Express se une a la Ripple Net". Criptonoticias. Accessed March 11, 2024, from https://www.criptonoticias.com/comunidad/adopcion/american-express-une-ripple-net/

[47] Ripple and Standard Chartered Bank (September 15, 2016). "Standard Chartered completes strategic investment in Ripple. Singapore. Accessed March 11, 2024, from https://www.sc.com/technology/assets/pdf/9-15-08-2016-Standard-Chartered-completes-strategic-investment-in-Ripple.pdf

distribution and use. Although XRP is traded on exchanges and can be used by individuals and businesses, its issuance and development are influenced by Ripple Labs' decisions.

In the case of Ripple, the absence of decentralization is clear. A system that is not fully decentralized, according to the principles of Internet Jurisdiction, can be more easily attacked by State Jurisdiction. When there is a visible company, headquarters, and management team, the State has a concrete target for supervision, taxation, and litigation, something that does not exist in the same way in fully decentralized projects such as Bitcoin. In fact, Ripple Labs has been involved in legal disputes with the U.S. Securities and Exchange Commission (SEC) over whether XRP should be considered an unregistered security, that is, stock market shares. On August 7, 2024, Ripple was convicted of violations of U.S. securities laws. For this, it must pay a civil fine of 125,035,150 dollars[48]. This has not happened with Bitcoin, for example, and until recently was the criterion followed with Ethereum for being decentralized, as stated by the SEC itself[49].

When a Digital Law is completely decentralized, no State can go after it, because it lacks a central entity.

---

[48] The sentence can be read here: https://assets.bwbx.io/documents/users/iqjWHBFdfxIU/royPDeTY0Ghc/v0

[49] For more information on this point, I recommend the BACS report "The SEC and Ethereum: Value or Commodity?" at https://bacsociety.com/wp-content/uploads/2023/10/EN-SEC-and-Ethereum-security-or-commodity.pdf

The United States, in these cases, cannot go after a company behind Bitcoin because it does not exist. Bitcoin and Ethereum in the United States have been considered commodities by the Commodity Futures Trading Commission (CFTC) and not as traded securities.

4.6. Dogecoin Digital Law (DOGE).

This Digital Law was issued in December 2013. It is relevant to understand a reality that is very present in this early stage of the blockchain world, which is gambling and speculation. It was created by Billy Markus and Jackson Palmer as a fun version of Bitcoin based on the popular Internet meme of the Doge, that is, a Shiba Inu dog.

It became popular due to its active community and its use in Internet memes. Elon Musk encouraged its use and helped grow its community and its value.

It indeed brought speed and timeliness in transactions, with lower expense per transaction compared to other cryptocurrencies. It served as one of the main alternatives for tips and artist collaborations in the digital world. In January 2014, Dogecoin became a commonly used currency for almost all Reddit users, numbering over 300 million[50].

Dogecoin, initially based on the source code of Litecoin, which in turn is based on Bitcoin, operates on

---

[50] Satoshitango (s.f.). "Aprende de Dogecoin". Accessed March 11, 2024, from https://www.satoshitango.com/criptomonedas/dogecoin

its own blockchain network, known as the Dogecoin network[51].

Although Dogecoin started as a joke, it quickly gained popularity in the crypto community and became one of the most well known and widely used cryptocurrencies.

Elon Musk began promoting Dogecoin in 2020 through his Twitter posts. Musk tweeted several times about Dogecoin, generating a surge in interest and price for the cryptocurrency. He has also praised Dogecoin's fun and friendly nature and suggested that it could become "the people's currency" or even "the currency of Mars".

Dogecoin also illustrates another reality of this early stage of crypto assets, namely that some influential figures take advantage of the situation to move markets and extract personal gain, leaving many latecomers exposed to abrupt price swings.

4.7. Monero (XMR) Digital Law.

This Digital Law was issued in April 2014. This proposal is very interesting because it regulates a payment system where payments are completely anonymous. Monero uses advanced privacy

---

[51] The Dogecoin network is a decentralized blockchain that uses a Proof of Work (PoW) consensus algorithm to validate and confirm transactions.

technologies[52] to offer completely private, anonymous, and untraceable transactions.

This was novel to the community because in other blockchains, such as Bitcoin or Ethereum, all transactions are public and pseudonymous. In these, the open and transparent nature of the blockchain allows anyone to track the flow of funds between addresses. It is also possible to link and analyze transactions and know the end user. For example, if a blockchain address is used to withdraw funds through an exchange that complies with Know Your Customer (KYC) regulations, the user's real identity could be associated with that address and all its transactions.

Monero (XMR) is the native cryptocurrency of this privacy-focused blockchain. Like other cryptocurrencies, Monero relies on a decentralized network of nodes that validate and confirm transactions on the blockchain. This ensures that the network is resistant to censorship and manipulation.

These types of blockchains that guarantee anonymity are a challenge to all State regulations regarding money laundering. State regulations prohibit regulated crypto asset service providers from operating these private blockchains. The exchange Binance has

---

[52] To ensure the privacy of the Monero network, it uses a combination of technologies such as ring signatures, Ring Confidential Transactions (RingCT), and stealth addresses. The purpose is to hide transaction information such as sender, recipient, and transaction amount. This ensures that transactions on the Monero network are private and untraceable.

already announced that it will stop offering Monero (XMR) on its platform[53].

Monero, therefore, sits at the center of a deep tension between the right to financial privacy and the desire of States to monitor flows of value to enforce tax, criminal, and regulatory rules.

---

[53] Pérez, H. (August 12, 2024). "Monero, Bitcóin Gold y otros tókenes se van de Binance en septiembre". Diario Bitcoin. Accessed August 19, 2024, from https://www.diariobitcoin.com/monero/monero-bitcoin-gold-y-otros-tokens-se-van-de-binance-en-septiembre/

4.8. Ethereum (ETH) Digital Law.

This Digital Law was issued in July 2015. It was proposed in 2013 by Vitalik Buterin and subsequently developed by a team of programmers.

Until Ethereum, anyone who wanted to issue their own Digital Law needed to create their own blockchain. Since the issuance of Ethereum Digital Law, anyone can easily issue their own Digital Law, in addition to an infinite number of applications, all from Ethereum's own blockchain. From a more technical point of view, Ethereum is a decentralized platform that allows the creation of smart contracts and decentralized applications (dApps). Its founding document, the whitepaper, is entitled "A Next Generation Smart Contract and Decentralized Application Platform"[54].

The difference between Ethereum and Bitcoin is that the latter is like a "dumb blockchain" that only allows sending and receiving Bitcoins[55]. Ethereum, on the other hand, is a "smart blockchain". Ethereum uses something like a decentralized computer or a decentralized virtual machine called the Ethereum Virtual Machine (EVM). This allows it to run smart contracts and decentralized applications (dApps). In

---

[54] Buterin, V. (2014). Ethereum Whitepaper.

[55] It is true that the Bitcoin blockchain is evolving to enable more applications such as decentralized finance (DeFi). One way to integrate DeFi on top of Bitcoin is through sidechains or Layer 2. Sidechains are blockchains that operate independently but are linked to the Bitcoin blockchain. Through sidechains, smart contracts are implemented that are not native to the Bitcoin blockchain, for example, DeFi applications. One of the best-known Bitcoin sidechains is the Lightning Network (LN).

practical terms, developers can program rules and conditions in code and deploy them so that they are executed automatically on thousands of nodes around the world without the need for a central server.

This has surely been the second most important legislative proposal after Bitcoin. The community has recognized this, and therefore, it is the second Digital Law in market capitalization.

Using State jurisdiction as a metaphor, Ethereum would be like an organic Digital Law that makes a decentralized legislator available to the community in order to issue its own Digital Laws.

The website Etherscan[56] provides us with a lot of Ethereum information. For example, we can know all the tokens, or Digital Laws, issued from this blockchain[57]: 1,327,247 tokens, or Digital Laws, have been issued on this blockchain, which is not too bad (see Fig. 5).

Finally, it should be noted that since the issuance of Ethereum Digital Law, other similar proposals have emerged that compete directly, such as Cardano (ADA), Solana (SOL), Polkadot (DOT), Avalanche (AVAX), Binance Smart Chain (BSC), Tezos (XTZ), Algorand (ALGO), or Cosmos (ATOM). Each of these platforms explores different trade-offs in scalability, security, fees, and governance, which shows how the

---

56 https://etherscan.io/

57 https://etherscan.io/tokens

market of Digital Laws behaves like a continuous laboratory of constitutional experiments on the Internet.

A total of 1,384,090 Token Contracts found

[illegible]

#	Token	Price	Change (%)	Volume (24H)	Circulating Market Cap	Onchain Market Cap	Holders
1	Tether USD (USDT)	$0.9997 [illegible]	-0.02%	$49,407,153,416.00	$119,594,573,641.00	$54,947,918,054.72	6,174,002 [illegible]
2	BNB (BNB)	$572.0417 [illegible]	-3.96%	$1,881,897,575.60	$83,479,676,462.00	$224,759,785.88	297,379 [illegible]
3	USDC (USDC)	$0.9998 [illegible]	0.01%	$5,154,071,930.00	$36,073,501,200.00	$20,806,490,297.49	2,344,826 [illegible]
4	XRP (IBC) (XRP)	$0.5295 [illegible]	0.33%	$3,206,429,705.00	$35,632,916,635.00	$5.30	3 [illegible]
5	stETH (stETH)	$2,601.47 [illegible]	-1.51%	$37,823,398.00	$23,529,961,240.00	$25,550,889,110.64	469,836 [illegible]
6	Wrapped TON Coin (TONCOIN)	$5.74 [illegible]	-1.15%	$283,713,122.00	$14,560,271,182.00	$68,695,623.18	93,097 [illegible]
7	Wrapped liquid staked ... (wstETH)	$3,066.58 [illegible]	-1.56%	$23,909,309.00	$10,808,795,303.00	$12,765,130,225.00	13,679 [illegible]
8	SHIBA INU (SHIB)	$0.00 [illegible]	-5.60%	$649,790,690.00	$10,761,305,529.00	$18,259,677,402.27	1,405,141 [illegible]
9	Wrapped BTC (WBTC)	$60,258.09 [illegible]	-3.27%	$155,549,373.00	$9,691,080,414.00	$9,670,946,298.00	101,678 [illegible]
10	Wrapped Ether (WETH)	$2,597.7473 [illegible]	-0.96%	$639,798,533.00	$8,852,821,190.00	$7,535,817,879.08	1,089,221 [illegible]
11	ChainLink Token (LINK)	$12.08 [illegible]	-3.98%	$347,638,474.00	$7,542,743,888.00	$12,030,800,000.00	721,455 [illegible]

Fig. 5.

Each of these platforms has its own advantages and disadvantages, and the choice between any of them depends on the specific needs of the project, including factors such as scalability, security, ease of development, and support community.

Ethereum remains one of the leading smart contract platforms due to its widespread adoption and developer community. However, these alternatives are gaining ground by offering innovative solutions to existing challenges related to blockchain technology.

4.9. Tether Digital Law (2014) and Genius Act (2025).

This Digital Law was issued in 2014. Cryptocurrencies have often been criticized for their volatility compared to fiat currencies such as the dollar or the euro. This argument is widely repeated by the official school of thought.

But it turns out that the community, as I have pointed out before, proposes effective solutions to real problems on its own initiative. One such problem was volatility. So a currency called a stablecoin [58] was issued. It is designed to maintain a stable value tied to the value of the U.S. dollar (USD). Since Bitcoin and Ethereum, to name the two most important assets, are very volatile, Tether offers the community a stable asset from which to trade other volatile digital assets.

Before issuing a stablecoin asset like Tether (USDT), abandoning Bitcoin[59] or Ethereum positions

[58] The term stablecoin is based on the assumption that the U.S. dollar is stable. Some criticize this term on the grounds that the dollar, as a fiat currency, tends to devalue due to the unlimited printing of this currency. This issue is not the subject of analysis here.

[59] Bitcoin's short-term value is like a roller coaster. From its inception in 2009 until the end of 2013, it experienced remarkable volatility and exponential growth in price. In 2010, the Bitcoin price closed the year at around 0.30 dollars. In 2011, Bitcoin experienced its first significant price bubble, reaching approximately 31 dollars in June before falling sharply to 2 dollars in November. Throughout 2012, Bitcoin's price slowly recovered from its 2011 plunge, closing the year around 13 dollars. That year was relatively stable compared to the volatility of the previous and subsequent years. The year 2013 was a year of extreme volatility for Bitcoin. The price started the year at around 13 dollars. In April, it reached a peak of approximately 260 dollars, followed by a rapid and significant drop. In October and November 2013, Bitcoin began another dramatic climb, reaching over 1,100 dollars in some markets in December before experiencing another significant correction.

required selling them to buy another volatile crypto asset. To settle on a stable position, it was necessary to switch from crypto to fiat, U.S. dollars, paying high fees. That is why the option of using a crypto asset associated with the value of the dollar has proved to be very practical.

Initially, Tether (USDT) was launched on the Bitcoin blockchain as a token based on the Omni Layer protocol[60]. However, over time, Tether has expanded to operate on several additional blockchains to take advantage of their unique features and capabilities. Currently, Tether is available on Ethereum, as an ERC 20 token, Tron, as a TRC 20 token, and others[61]. Tether is currently the third-largest cryptocurrency by market capitalization behind Bitcoin and Ethereum. In the chart above, Tether is listed as the most important cryptocurrency in the Ethereum network.

In addition to Tether, other Digital Laws have been issued that regulate stable currencies such as USD Coin (USDC)[62], Binance USD (BUSD) in derogation[63],

---

[60] Omni Layer is a layer built on top of the Bitcoin blockchain that enables the issuance and exchange of digital tokens using smart contracts.

[61] Each version of Tether on a different blockchain has its own unique identifier, for example, USDT ETH for Tether on Ethereum or USDT TRX for Tether on Tron.

[62] Issued by Circle.

[63] A stablecoin backed by the U.S. dollar and issued by Binance in partnership with Paxos. As announced by Binance, it recommended the community stop using this crypto asset by February 2024.

BUSD[64], Dai (DAI)[65], TrueUSD (TUSD)[66], Paxos Standard (PAX)[67], and Gemini Dollar (GUSD)[68].

Taken together, these projects show how the Internet Jurisdiction has created its own toolbox of digital dollars, each with different degrees of decentralization, regulatory oversight, and technological design.

In this context, the "Guiding and Establishing National Innovation for U.S. Stablecoins Act" (GENIUS Act), enacted as Public Law 119 27 on July 18, 2025, represents the first comprehensive federal law in the world to create and regulate U.S. dollar stablecoins[69].

Stablecoin issuers must maintain 1:1 reserves for each stablecoin issued. These reserves can be held in physical currency, U.S. Treasury bills, repurchase agreements, and other low-risk assets approved by regulators. Issuers are required to report on the composition of reserves and are subject to periodic

---

64 It seeks to offer a reliable and regulated alternative to Tether, with the approval of financial regulators.

65 Dai is a decentralized stablecoin backed by cryptocurrencies instead of fiat money. It is issued by MakerDAO.

66 TrueUSD is focused on transparency and security. It is often audited to confirm that it has full dollar backing.

67 Now known as Pax Dollar (USDP), it is a stablecoin issued by Paxos. Like USDC and BUSD, it seeks to offer transparency and security in its operations.

68 Issued by the Gemini cryptocurrency exchange, co-founded by the Winklevoss twins.

69 Public Law 119-27 (Jul. 18, 2025), *Guiding and Establishing National Innovation for U.S. Stablecoins Act*, codified at 139 Stat. 419.

audits by registered public accounting firms [70]. In practice, this turns each regulated stablecoin into a kind of narrow bank deposit fully backed by short-term sovereign or cash equivalent assets rather than by risky loans.

These currencies are expected to be on the market by January 2027.

This move has not gone unnoticed by other countries around the world. The European Union has confirmed its intention to create a CBDC or "digital euro." Meanwhile, Russia has pointed out that the United States wants to erase a 35 trillion dollar debt with cryptocurrencies[71]. For the first time, monetary competition is emerging not only between central banks but also between different designs of digital dollars and digital sovereign currencies.

We cannot predict how many millions of dollars will be issued under the GENIUS Act. Today, in 2025, we have a stablecoin market cap of 313 billion dollars issued by six major issuers. That gives an average of 40 to 50 billion dollars per issuer.

Under the GENIUS Act, the new regulatory framework for stablecoins in the United States, there could be around 50 state issuers, each with a

---

[70] Genius Act sec 4 (a) (1) (A) and World Economic Forum, July 29, 2025. Accessed 15 December 2025. URL: https://www.weforum.org/stories/2025/07/stablecoin-regulation-genius-act/

[71] Crypticke (09.10.2025). "Asesor de Putín: EE.UU. planea borrar una deuda de 35 billones de dólares con criptomonedas". Bidget. Accessed December 12th, 2025. https://www.bitget.com/es/news/detail/12560604958896

maximum issuance of 10 billion dollars, along with 10 large-scale federal issuers with an average issuance of around 200 billion dollars each.

Added to this would be international expansion, estimated at between 2 trillion and 4 trillion dollars, which would bring the total potential issuance of stablecoins to around 6 trillion dollars by the end of the decade, with aggressive scenarios exceeding 10 trillion dollars. These are illustrative projections, not certainties, but they show the possible order of magnitude of dollar tokenization if the GENIUS framework is widely adopted at home and abroad.

This expansion of regulated liquidity would make stablecoins the core of the new digital monetary system, boosting the total capitalization of the crypto market to levels close to 40 trillion dollars. In this context, if Bitcoin maintains its historical dominance of 50 percent, its capitalization could reach 20 trillion dollars, which would put its theoretical price at around 1 million dollars per unit.

If the total market cap of the crypto ecosystem increases tenfold, from 4 trillion dollars to 40 trillion dollars, driven by the expansion of regulated stablecoins under the GENIUS Act, and Bitcoin retains a 50 percent dominance, the theoretical price of Bitcoin would be around 1 million dollars per unit by 2029.

Added to these forecasts is a structural factor: Bitcoin's fifth halving, scheduled for April 2028, which will reduce the block issuance from 3.125 to 1.5625 BTC, limiting daily creation to just 225 BTC. This event will reduce the annual new supply to below 82,000 BTC, intensifying scarcity just as global digital liquidity expands because of the GENIUS Act.

Together, these two processes, regulated digital monetary expansion and the programmed contraction of Bitcoin supply, outline a possible decade of structural revaluation of the Internet's sovereign asset, with the potential to place Bitcoin between 1 million and 2 million dollars per unit by 2029–2030.

These forecasts seem moderate compared to the forecast by Larry Fink, CEO of BlackRock, who predicts a market cap of 15 trillion dollars[72].

---

[72] Social media X https://x.com/MerlijnTrader/status/1975093668332597255

5. State Jurisdiction, French Revolution, and Industrial Revolution

Earlier, I explained that with Bitcoin, a new global and decentralized jurisdiction has emerged, which I call the Internet Jurisdiction. It stands in contrast to the traditional jurisdiction of the State, which is local and rooted in physical territory. Within its borders, the State exercises its legal power[73] over persons, property, and situations that occur there.

From the perspective of the Internet Jurisdiction, the State is a second-layer, external actor. It can only attempt to regulate the effects of the Internet Jurisdiction within its territory or over its nationals[74].

A brief look at recent history shows how the power of the State has expanded to exaggerated limits, far beyond what earlier societies would have considered acceptable.

That power rests on the concept of "sovereignty", which crystallized after the Peace of Westphalia in 1648, the treaty that ended the Thirty Years' War[75] and

---

[73] The power of the State is legal, accepted by all or by the majority; the clearest proof is that many people continue to vote in elections, which shows they still believe in the legality of the system.

[74] In the case of the United States, the government applies principles of extraterritorial jurisdiction: agencies such as the SEC can take regulatory and enforcement actions against U.S. citizens, companies, or anyone doing business with them, regardless of residence or geographic location.

[75] The Thirty Years' War (1618–1648) was a devastating conflict that involved much of Europe and combined religious struggles between Catholics and Protestants with competition for political and territorial power. The Peace of

the Eighty Years' War[76]. From that moment, a new political and religious order was established in Europe. The treaty is regarded as a milestone in European and world history because it laid the foundations for the modern system of international relations and State sovereignty.

Once this power structure had been consolidated, it had to be sold to the "subjects". This is where numerous "intellectual" theories appeared, often presented as if ideas came first and power later, when in reality history suggests the opposite: first comes power (and technology), and only afterwards the ideology that justifies them.

One of the great legal theories of the modern State is the so-called "social contract"[77]. European philosophers of the 17th and 18th centuries developed the idea that sovereignty rests on an implicit, rather than express, contractual relationship between individuals and the State. In other words, when we are born, besides receiving a slap from the midwife, we

Westphalia ended the war and recognized State sovereignty and religious freedom.

[76] The Eighty Years' War (1568–1648) was a conflict between Spain and the Netherlands, which sought independence from Spanish rule. The Peace of Westphalia also ended this war and recognized the independence of the Netherlands.

[77] The core ideas behind the social contract were developed by philosophers such as Thomas Hobbes, John Locke, and Jean-Jacques Rousseau. Although they shared the basic concept, they differed significantly on its implications and on the nature of the agreement.

supposedly enter a contract with the State, of which we are unaware but which binds us to "society"[78].

Some movements, such as anarchism and certain libertarian currents, have denied that such an agreement was ever freely accepted[79]. Nevertheless, the concept of the social contract has been central to justifying political authority, legitimizing government, and grounding modern theories of human rights and social justice.

Bitcoin's sovereign power is not ideological but factual and technical. Bitcoin does not sell theory; it simply operates as a digital law that produces concrete effects within the Internet Jurisdiction.

Secondly, State power found two great historical allies: the French Revolution of 1789 and the Industrial Revolution. The French Revolution centralized power not in a monarch but in the State itself. The institution around which medieval life revolved, the Catholic Church, was gradually displaced by a new figure: the secular State.

A civic cult of the nation emerged, expressed in flags, anthems, and other symbols of belonging. The

---

[78] The implicit (or unconscious) social-contract agreement still in force today has far-reaching consequences: individuals voluntarily yield certain rights and freedoms to a central power in exchange for protection and preservation of social order.

[79] Some authors argue that simply registering a newborn in the civil registry may amount to tacit acceptance of the social contract. In practice, however, non-registration is rarely a viable option.

modern notions of "citizen" and "nationality" were born in this context.

If in the Middle Ages life revolved around religion, from 1789 onwards, moral obligations were linked to the homeland and the nation. The individual exchanged the altar for the State, and then for the trench. He no longer gave his life for the faith, but for the homeland.

The concept of "citizen" is particularly interesting. Simon Schama develops it in his work Citizens. Before the Revolution, France was structured around a monarchical and feudal system in which most people were subjects with limited rights under the rule of the king. The French Revolution, with its ideals of liberty, equality, and fraternity, sought to transform this reality by establishing a society where all men and women were considered equal citizens before the law. This equality is conceptual, but not real.

On the other hand, the Internet is technically a platform based on peer-to-peer relationships. On the Internet, equality is not promised as an ideal; it is simply exercised in practice by anyone who connects.

The State also benefited from the Industrial Revolution. Thanks to steady economic growth, a larger middle class emerged. Poverty was reduced, the population increased, and the "masses" appeared. In particular, mass democracy, mass armies, mass education, mass communication, and mass consumer products were born.

The best news for the modern State was the factual possibility of directing these national masses. Part of the population (mainly men) worked in factories, from which they did not move. Another part (mainly women) stayed at home. This configuration made it easier for the State to control entrepreneurs and, therefore, workers.

Let us think about it: in feudal times, the Lord or King had to negotiate with many intermediaries (for example, counts or lords) before reaching the final subject. The modern State eliminated these medieval intermediaries (who were also privileged and therefore not equal) to control citizens directly.

The State gained the advantage of being able to control millions of people who were officially "equals". That is why taxes such as income tax and many other extractive taxes arose. The State continued to grow and expand its power until the Technological Revolution and the Internet. Now, with the Internet, the State is getting a taste of its own medicine.

Bitcoin and the rest of the Digital Laws are eliminating State intermediaries known as "trusted third parties", which are not equal either. They do so through networks of relationships based on equality, where any node can decide with whom to interact and on what terms, irrespective of past hierarchies.

To conclude this section, and from a legal point of view, the jurisdiction of the State covers a wide range of areas, including mainly:

1. Civil and commercial jurisdiction.

This includes the authority of the State to regulate and resolve disputes between private parties. Some examples are contracts between private parties, the exercise of property rights, and matters related to family law, such as separations, divorces, and custody of children.

The way some of these rights are exercised is changing with the issuance and application of new Digital Laws. For example, the exercise of ownership rights in crypto-assets is no longer based on the "registered owner" but on possession of the access keys to the wallet. This already leads to major problems, such as identifying the actual owner of the crypto-assets.

In the case of inheritances, lawyers can start preparing, because "crypto-litigation" is assured. For example, who really has access to Tom's wallet, who, because of his grandson, bought 1,000 Bitcoins in 2012?

Tom, despite having been a good father and faithful husband, was abandoned in a nursing home by his relatives. He is cared for by Dick, a person as strong-willed as he is short-minded. In his village, he was called "the sharp one, and not exactly because of his intellectual capacity.

Every morning, Tom repeats the same old rant he always does. But one day, while watching the news on TV, they talked about Bitcoin. A distant light bulb lights up in Tom's bald head, which he occasionally shows when he takes off his beret.

He comments to his new friend Dick that he has that "rare coin" somewhere and that he barely invested 1,000 dollars back in 2012, money he assumes to be lost. Dick, despite his limited intellectual resources, knows how to do one thing: search the Internet.

With the 2012 price of Bitcoin and 1,000 dollars of investment, he does the math. All his ingenious plans to become Tom's universal heir by legal means are immediately discarded. There is a new objective: to obtain the keys to the old man's Bitcoins.

Similarly, the way rights and obligations are represented is changing with tokenization. Primarily, this trend has been empowered, as noted earlier, since the issuance of the Ethereum Digital Law. This will mean a new way of organizing ourselves in law, as I explain in more detail in Chapter 3.

At the moment, real estate, commercial companies, movable assets, jewelry, works of art, and many other assets are being tokenized. Just as children gather in the school yard to exchange trading cards, adults will increasingly gather in digital spaces to exchange tokens that embody rights and obligations.

Many of the legal solutions that have been applied for centuries are no longer capable of adequately addressing the needs presented by artificial intelligence, crypto-assets, new technologies, and, ultimately, the Internet. The system is outdated. I reflect further on this in Chapters 2 and 3.

2. Criminal jurisdiction.

This comprises the power of the State to investigate, prosecute, and punish crimes occurring within its territory or perpetrated by its nationals. This jurisdiction will continue to be exercised by whoever represents the power that is legally established and recognized by the community.

3. Administrative jurisdiction.

This implies the authority of the State to regulate and make decisions on matters related to the administration of the State itself, such as permits, licenses, or taxes, among others. This privilege of the State will diminish as its powers are reduced.

From a conceptual point of view, an administrative law of crypto-assets does not yet exist, at least for the time being, because they are private initiatives.

4. International jurisdiction

This refers to the capacity of the State to represent itself and exercise its authority in international affairs, including treaties, diplomatic relations, and disputes between States[80]. Internet Jurisdiction, by contrast, is universal and operates without the need for States.

---

[80] The word "international" was coined by Jeremy Bentham in 1789, the same year as the French Revolution. In the Internet age, the concept of the nation is becoming less central; relations are increasingly "extra-national".

6. Internet Jurisdiction

Internet Jurisdiction is based on decentralization. Sovereignty is not hierarchical, but peer-to-peer. It does not rely on "the people" or on national citizens, but on anyone, anywhere in the world.

From Bitcoin onwards, it has been possible to relate as equals with people from all over the world in order to do business, transmit information, and transfer value regardless of race, nation, gender, socio-economic level, or faith. This is the opposite of the organization built around the State.

The prelude to the Internet was the development of computers. One of the great precursors was the Englishman Alan Turing, who in 1936 published his work "On Computable Numbers, with an Application to the Entscheidungsproblem"[81].

His work was fundamental for the theory of computation and influenced the development of modern computers and our understanding of what can and cannot be computed by algorithms.

Ethereum Digital Law, among others, uses a kind of "decentralized computer" called the Ethereum Virtual Machine (EVM). The EVM builds on Turing's computational framework and enables decentralized computing to execute smart contracts. Bitcoin, on the

[81] Alan Turing, "On Computable Numbers, with an Application to the Entscheidungsproblem" (1936).

other hand, is not "Turing-complete"[82], which is why some people refer to it as a "dumb blockchain".

It is curious that the computational method of modern computers arose in what used to be the world's pre-eminent power, the United Kingdom, while the Internet emerged from the new world power, the United States.

The Internet was the result of a series of technological and conceptual developments that took place over several decades. In the 1960s, the first version of the Internet began with the creation of ARPANET, a communications network funded by the U.S. Department of Defense's Advanced Research Projects Agency (ARPA). ARPA wanted to create a communications network that could continue to function even if some connections were lost – for example, in the event of a nuclear attack – and that would also save costs by sharing information between several computers simultaneously.

ARPANET went live in 1969, initially connecting four institutions: the University of California at Los Angeles (UCLA), the Stanford Research Institute (SRI), the University of California at Santa Barbara (UCSB), and the University of Utah. Over time, that experimental network evolved into today's Internet, a

[82] By limiting the computational power of its scripting language, Bitcoin keeps the network more robust and easier to audit. The language only supports a restricted set of operations that is sufficient for transferring value but not for complex computation.

global infrastructure that few of its creators could have imagined.

The book Where Wizards Stay Up Late: The Origins of the Internet recounts the early history and development of the network, focusing especially on the creation of ARPANET, the forerunner of today's global network. Hafner and Lyon describe how a small group of engineers, scientists, and visionaries worked under the auspices of ARPA. These little-remembered heroes collaborated to build the first large-scale computer network using packet switching as the fundamental technique for data communication[83].

In 1983, ARPANET adopted the TCP/IP (Transmission Control Protocol/Internet Protocol) suite, developed by Vinton Cerf and Robert Kahn. This adoption marked the birth of the Internet as a global "network of networks" because TCP/IP made it possible to interconnect disparate networks and transmit data in a uniform, reliable way.

Throughout the 1980s and early 1990s, other networks joined and expanded, including academic and research networks such as NSFNET (National Science Foundation Network) in the United States and many international networks. They also adopted TCP/IP, which facilitated their interconnection with ARPANET and with each other.

---

[83] Among the figures highlighted in Where Wizards Stay Up Late are J. C. R. Licklider, Robert Taylor, Lawrence Roberts, Paul Baran, Vint Cerf, and many others whose ideas, research, and leadership were crucial.

In 1989, Tim Berners-Lee, a computer scientist at CERN (the European Organization for Nuclear Research), invented the World Wide Web (WWW). The Web provided a simple, unified way to access information on the Internet using graphical browsers. It used the HTTP (Hypertext Transfer Protocol) to transmit data and HTML (Hypertext Markup Language) to structure web pages.

Thanks to all these contributions, we can enjoy the Internet today.

A highly topical book, given the challenges we face, is Crypto: How the Code Rebels Beat the Government, Saving Privacy in the Digital Age [84]. Steven Levy recounts the struggle of cryptographers who developed and distributed strong encryption tools to protect individual privacy.

On the other side was the U.S. government, which sought to control and limit the use of cryptography for national security reasons. Germany had used the famous Enigma machine during World War II to encrypt all its military messages. Alan Turing played a crucial role in decoding the encrypted messages generated by that machine – a contribution that helped the Allies win the war.

For the authors of The Sovereign Individual, it is no coincidence that the world's dominant power, the United States, tried to control and limit cryptography in

---

[84] Levy, S. (2002). Crypto: How the Code Rebels Beat the Government, Saving Privacy in the Digital Age. Alianza.

much the same way that the Catholic Church – the predominant institution of the 15th century – tried to control knowledge when the printing press appeared[85]. In both cases, technology threatened forms of government that were becoming obsolete: bureaucratic, hyper-regulated systems with high taxes and major obstacles to trade.

The United States, and specifically the NSA (National Security Agency), kept tight control over cryptography. It supervised all patent applications related to cryptography and was authorized by law to classify as secret any idea that seemed too dangerous to be in the public domain[86].

The U.S. government's fear was not unfounded. An outsider who understood the country's encryption systems might be able to design their own codes or launch digital attacks.

But it was not just cryptography that was treated as a matter of national security. The scientists and mathematicians who developed it also raised questions that affect us directly today: wouldn't people themselves need to protect their communications and personal data from any intruder, including the

---

[85] Davidson, J. D. and Rees-Mogg, W. (2022). The Sovereign Individual: Mastering the Transition to the Information Age (chapter 4, "The Last Days of Politics"). Bubok Publishing: Kindle edition.

[86] Levy, S. (2002). Crypto: How the Code Rebels Beat the Government, Saving Privacy in the Digital Age. Alianza.

government? Doesn't everyone have a right to privacy?[87]

Levy describes the contributions of several key figures in the field of cryptography. Their work laid part of the groundwork for Bitcoin, which uses some of these discoveries.

Whitfield Diffie and Martin Hellman, for example, published the article "New Directions in Cryptography" in 1976, where they introduced the concept of public-key cryptography and the Diffie–Hellman key-exchange protocol. This protocol allows two parties to generate a shared secret key over an insecure channel without having previously exchanged any secrets. It was a revolutionary breakthrough. Public-key cryptography is essential for cryptocurrencies, including Bitcoin, because it enables secure transactions.

Ralph Merkle contributed to the development of public-key cryptography with his concept of cryptographic puzzles. In 1974, he proposed "Merkle trees", fundamental data structures for organizing large data sets. Merkle trees make it possible to verify the integrity of large bodies of data efficiently and are an integral part of blockchain technology, the basis of Bitcoin.

---

[87] Ibid. Prologue.

Ron Rivest, Adi Shamir, and Leonard Adleman developed the RSA algorithm, the first practical public-key cryptography system.

Levy also recounts various confrontations between cryptographers and the U.S. government. Because of the struggle of these "code rebels, public-key cryptography has become an integral part of the Internet's security infrastructure. Thanks to their work, we can protect our data, from personal communications to global financial transactions.

However, it will be up to our generation to keep the torch of privacy and freedom lit. States are now attempting to extend their control to virtually unlimited levels, this time through digital monetary infrastructures.

This is where the so-called "CBDC" currencies come in[88]. They are digital currencies issued by States and recorded on a blockchain in a centralized manner. The initiative does not distinguish between left- or right-wing governments, democracies, or authoritarian regimes: all States seek to protect their own interests in the face of the new era of decentralization.

The effects of CBDCs could be devastating for citizens' privacy and freedom. Imagine trying to pay your restaurant bill and having the payment rejected because you have already consumed more meat than the latest public-health and environmental guidelines

[88] CBDC stands for Central Bank Digital Currency.

allow. Or imagine that your CBDC balance disappears if it is not spent within a certain time, according to the most recent directive on economic "stimulus". These and many other controls would be technically possible with CBDCs. This is not science fiction: in Thailand, for example, a "digital wallet" program has been trialed in which money can only be spent within a limited perimeter around the user's home[89].

Some may think this view is exaggerated, but Christine Lagarde, President of the European Central Bank, has herself dispelled many doubts. In a secretly recorded conversation with a prankster posing as President Zelensky, she acknowledged that "the digital euro will be used to control people and payments, and added that "we are considering whether, for very small amounts, around 300 or 400 euros, we could have a zero-control mechanism. But that could be dangerous"[90].

Even the U.S. Congress has described the CBDC project as a tool to enable "stricter oversight of financial transactions"[91]. Some institutions are already warning publicly about this imminent risk.

---

[89] Jason Tam, T. (17 April 2024). "Should Thailand's Digital Wallet Policy Be Implemented?" Spheres of Influence. Also referenced by Dejanira Silveira on X (formerly Twitter) with video evidence of geofenced spending. Jason Tam, T. (17 abril 2024). Video was published in https://x.com/dejanirasilveir/status/1841911941381472 647, later deleted.

[90] Huigsloot, L. (7 April 2023). "CBDC will be used for 'control,' ECB president admits in video chat with fake Zelensky", Cointelegraph.

[91] U.S. Congress, "Central Bank Digital Currency", Congressional Research Service (CRS), 4 October 2024.

The Cato Institute points out that, aside from the basic programmability a CBDC would offer for social and political control, one of its most common features would be the ability to apply positive or negative interest rates in order to slow or stimulate purchases[92].

Similarly, the Competitive Enterprise Institute has warned that CBDCs could provide governments with a powerful instrument of economic and social control and an unprecedented intrusion into the private financial lives of billions of people[93].

If we do nothing, George Orwell's novel 1984 will become a fulfilled prophecy – and not in a communist country, but in the heart of the West.

Some of the crypto rebels of the 1960s and 1970s proposed the idea of "crypto-anarchy", summarized in Timothy C. May's 1988 "Crypto-Anarchist Manifesto"[94]. The manifesto advocates the use of cryptography and information technology to protect privacy and individual freedom in the digital age. May and other cypherpunks believed strongly in online privacy and in resisting government surveillance and control.

The manifesto underlined the transformative potential that new technologies could have on people's

---

[92] The Cato Institute has published several analyses warning that CBDCs could become tools for granular financial surveillance and behavioural control.

[93] Jossey, P. (2 February 2022). "A Government Central Bank Digital Currency Would Pose Big Risk to Financial Sector, Economy", Competitive Enterprise Institute.

[94] May, T. C. (1988). "The Crypto-Anarchist Manifesto".

lives and freedoms. At its core, it is also a legal statement: a prediction that strong encryption would make it possible to exchange information and value beyond the reach of traditional state control.

The relationship between the cypherpunk movement and Bitcoin is deeply significant and reflects a strong overlap of ideals. Cyberpunks advocated the use of technology to promote privacy, individual freedom, and decentralization, opposing both government and corporate intrusion into people's private lives. Bitcoin embodies many of these principles by offering a decentralized, pseudonymous, and censorship-resistant monetary system.

This was the intellectual and technological environment out of which Bitcoin emerged. As the community grows, however, two antagonistic worlds increasingly collide. A good example is Ripple, a project that uses blockchain technology to improve transactions between traditional financial institutions.

Little by little, the initial rebellious vision of crypto-assets is giving way to a more pragmatic use of the technology, seeking solutions that may benefit everyone. Prominent figures in traditional finance are already positioning themselves in favor of this new digital monetary ecosystem.

7. Relationship between State Jurisdiction and Internet Jurisdiction

Relations between States are a central element of classic international law. In theory, each State must respect the sovereignty and authority of others within its own borders and avoid interfering in their internal affairs.

In the case of relations between States and the Internet, the situation is very different. The Internet is not a centralized entity; here I refer specifically to the Internet Jurisdiction, understood as the decentralized network where legal effects are produced outside State structures.

The State is a centralized entity based on a clearly defined hierarchy and a unified system of government. The Internet, by contrast, has no central authority or single point of control. It is made up of a vast number of servers, networks, and devices distributed around the world, with multiple access points. No single entity can control the entire network.

In a centralized State, the government has significant control over almost every aspect of public life, including legislation, law enforcement, the economy, and public services. On the Internet, governance is more complex and distributed. There is no single authority that controls all aspects of the network. Instead, Internet governance involves multiple stakeholders: governments, companies, non-profit organizations, and individual users.

State power is based on sovereignty, recognized both by other States and by national citizens themselves. In the case of the Internet, sovereignty is exercised in a decentralized manner. This is precisely the true power of the Internet: its decentralization.

In a first phase, the Internet cannot easily be captured by States precisely because of its decentralized nature. The greater the decentralization, the greater the sovereignty and independence of Internet-based jurisdictions. The less decentralization, the less sovereignty – and the easier it becomes for States to intervene and challenge the Internet Jurisdiction.

In a second phase, the community will gradually become more aware of the power of the Internet and of its capacity to issue its own Digital Laws. This new role carries greater individual responsibility (no longer delegated to a central entity) and, with it, a personal sovereignty largely absent in recent centuries. Individuals will be able to choose between an outdated, bureaucratic, slow, and expensive system, or, on the contrary, voluntary submission to a wide range of agile, effective, and inexpensive legal systems governed by the community itself. In this second phase, decentralization will no longer be the only defense against State interference: society itself, transformed into a community, will actively support the Internet Jurisdiction.

One of the best examples of the power of decentralization is peer-to-peer (P2P) networks, which allow users to exchange resources such as files directly with each other without relying on central servers. A good illustration is BitTorrent, a protocol that enables file sharing at global scale. To date, BitTorrent has not been successfully censored by State jurisdictions.

The State can only act directly on Bitcoin within its national territory, but not in the Internet Jurisdiction as a whole. Bitcoin might have been defeated during its early years, when there were very few nodes supporting the system. But as the community grew, Bitcoin became sovereign and practically unbreakable.

Bitcoin was also designed to attract more community. In its early years, anyone tempted to attack the system would usually find it more profitable to join the network as a miner and earn Bitcoins than to try to undermine the blockchain and receive nothing in return. Bitcoin's design is therefore positive-sum. First, it attracts more nodes that support the network and receive rewards in Bitcoin. With more miners, the network becomes more robust. Finally, the stronger the system, the more users and nodes will join and support it. For this reason, and because the total number of Bitcoins is capped at 21 million and periodically reduced through "halving" events, the value of the asset tends to increase as adoption grows[95].

---

[95] Bitcoin's monetary policy combines a fixed maximum supply of 21 million coins with periodical "halving" events that reduce the block-reward over time, making the asset structurally scarce.

There are many other decentralized mechanisms on the Internet: decentralized messaging systems[96], decentralized social networks[97], decentralized domain-name systems[98], protocols such as the Interplanetary File System (IPFS), which allow content to be stored and distributed in a decentralized way[99], and instant-messaging and chat protocols that can also be implemented without central servers[100].

Some States have recognized, within their own jurisdictions, certain legal effects of applications that operate entirely in the Internet Jurisdiction.

First, States can issue legal norms that validate, recognize, and attribute legal effects to Digital Laws created in the Internet Jurisdiction. The clearest case is El Salvador, which passed the "Bitcoin Law" in June 2021, recognizing Bitcoin as legal tender[101]. This statute, issued from a State jurisdiction, recognizes

---

[96] Some decentralized messaging projects use end-to-end encryption and distributed infrastructure to protect user privacy and resist censorship. RetroShare is one example.

[97] Several decentralized social-network projects seek to avoid central servers and give users control over their data. Diaspora is one of the early attempts in this direction.

[98] Alternative, decentralized domain-name systems such as Handshake or Unstoppable Domains aim to reduce dependence on traditional registries and naming authorities.

[99] The InterPlanetary File System (IPFS) stores files in multiple locations instead of on a central server, using content-addressed hashes to ensure data integrity.

[100] Protocols such as Matrix or XMPP (Jabber) allow decentralized instant messaging and chat, enabling communication across different services and servers.

[101] "Ley Bitcoin" (Bitcoin Law), Official Gazette of El Salvador, June 2021.

and regulates within its territory the legal effects of a digital currency created in the Internet Jurisdiction.

Article 1 of that law states that its purpose is to regulate Bitcoin as legal tender with liberating power in any transaction and in any capacity that natural or legal persons, public or private, need to carry out. However, under pressure from the International Monetary Fund, El Salvador withdrew Bitcoin's status as legal tender on 30 January 2025[102].

Second, a State can regulate and recognize as legal a "financial product" whose underlying assets are crypto-assets. A clear example is Bitcoin or Ethereum ETFs (exchange-traded funds). ETFs are investment funds that trade on stock exchanges like shares. They allow investors to buy and sell participations that represent ownership of Bitcoin or Ethereum without directly holding the cryptocurrency. These funds give investors a more accessible and regulated way to gain exposure to cryptocurrencies.

The first Bitcoin ETF was approved in Canada on 18 February 2021. It is the Purpose Bitcoin ETF, which trades on the Toronto Stock Exchange (TSX) under the symbols BTCC.B and BTCC.U.

Since then, several other Bitcoin and Ethereum ETFs have been approved in different jurisdictions, including Europe and, more recently, the United States. On 10 January 2024, the U.S. Securities and

---

[102] Maximiliano Pérez Gallardo, "El Salvador retira el bitcoin como moneda de curso legal ante presiones del FMI", France 24, 31 January 2025.

Exchange Commission (SEC) approved the first spot Bitcoin ETFs, a milestone that brought large institutional capital into the sector.

The approval of Bitcoin and Ethereum ETFs marked an important step in recognizing, within State jurisdictions, the effects of digital assets that operate primarily in the Internet Jurisdiction. Crypto-asset purists criticize ETFs as a way of accessing a decentralized digital currency through a highly centralized financial product.

But in practice, many on-ramps to the crypto world already pass through centralized exchanges that swap fiat money for cryptocurrencies. In my view, the more entities, States and institutions that bet – even partially – on this new world, the better. Peaceful coexistence between both systems is the best guarantee that we are on the right path.

8. State Interference in the Jurisdiction of the Internet

Not all Digital Laws are fully decentralized – that is, not all of them are fully sovereign. At present, the only truly decentralized digital asset is Bitcoin.

States play two particularly relevant roles in relation to the Internet Jurisdiction. First, they oscillate between prohibition, strict control, and promotion of crypto-assets. Very restrictive policies can mean losing technological leadership. Second, they can impose heavy penalties on intermediaries, which in practice allows them to interfere with activities that take place in the Internet Jurisdiction.

With regard to regulation, some jurisdictions are clearly betting on encouraging blockchain technology, cryptocurrencies, and artificial intelligence. El Salvador, for instance, took the step of recognizing Bitcoin as legal tender. Other jurisdictions such as the United Arab Emirates [103], Singapore, Hong Kong, Kazakhstan, Bahrain, and Qatar are also adopting measures to attract companies in these sectors.

By contrast, the United States has often relied more on enforcement than on clear rules. In June 2023, for example, the U.S. exchange Coinbase was sued by the Securities and Exchange Commission

[103] Dubai, in particular, is positioning itself as a technological hub for blockchain, crypto-assets, and artificial-intelligence projects.

(SEC) for allegedly trading crypto-assets classified as securities. While Coinbase was being punished by its own regulator, Hong Kong publicly invited the company to operate from its territory and serve global markets[104].

The European Union has approved the Markets in Crypto-Assets (MiCA) regulation, a positive step because it harmonizes crypto-asset rules across the Union.

The case of the United States is noteworthy. It led the development of the "Internet of information" in the 1990s, giving birth to companies such as Amazon, Facebook, Google, Apple, and Microsoft. The same is not happening with the "Internet of value", based on blockchain and crypto-assets.

J. Christopher Giancarlo, former chairman of the Commodity Futures Trading Commission (CFTC) and one of the great promoters of blockchain technology in the United States, has become known as "Crypto Dad"[105]. In various interviews, he has reflected on the U.S. role and its challenges in the coming years.

Giancarlo points out that in the 1990s, the United States passed the right laws to support innovation on the Internet. Such a regulatory step has not yet been taken in the world of crypto-assets, forcing many

---

[104] Nwaokocha, A. (11 June 2023). "Hong Kong legislator invites Coinbase to the region despite SEC scrutiny", Cointelegraph.

[105] J. Christopher Giancarlo, CryptoDad: The Fight for the Future of Money, Wiley, 2021.

leading companies to establish themselves in tax-friendly jurisdictions[106]. He argues that the U.S. lacks clear regulation for these new technologies, unlike other regions such as the European Union with MiCA. In his view, the country is wasting energy talking about scandals while ignoring the key issue: the underlying technology.

For Giancarlo, one of the biggest contributions of crypto-assets is that they allow value to be stored and transmitted natively on the Internet. This implies a new financial architecture that is open, fast, and efficient. Put simply, value – understood as rights of ownership or use – is no longer recorded only in physical registries but also in global digital ledgers. With Bitcoin and similar systems, a new legal architecture is being created that is global, rapid, and highly resilient[107].

Giancarlo also stresses the need for good regulation by competent authorities such as the SEC and the CFTC. For him, it is necessary to prevent the scandals that always accompany new technologies, but it is even more important to adapt to innovation. Regulation must adapt to technology, not the other way around.

---

[106] Paul Barron Network. (June 21, 2023). Former CFTC Chris Giancarlo interview / Fast tracking Crypto regulation vs SEC (min. 19).

[107] Giancarlo has repeatedly argued that, just as the United States created the legal framework that enabled the early Internet to flourish, it now needs a clear and innovation-friendly framework for digital assets.

States can also interfere by imposing sanctions on more centralized entities that provide services related to the Internet Jurisdiction.

The U.S. authorities have targeted major exchanges. These private companies are the main gateway to the cryptocurrency world because they convert fiat money into crypto-assets. In addition to Coinbase, the most spectacular case has been Binance.

Binance was founded in 2017 by Changpeng Zhao ("CZ") and quickly became the world's largest exchange by trading volume. The platform offers a wide range of services, including spot trading, futures, staking, and more.

In 2019, Binance launched "Binance US" as a separate legal entity intended to comply with U.S. regulations. However, the SEC later sued Binance US for alleged violations of securities-market rules.

In November 2023, Binance and its CEO, Changpeng Zhao, reached a major settlement with several U.S. agencies, including the Department of Justice (DOJ), the Commodity Futures Trading Commission (CFTC), and the Financial Crimes Enforcement Network (FinCEN). Binance agreed to pay a total of 4.3 billion dollars in fines for various violations of U.S. law, including willful evasion of money-laundering rules and the illegal operation of a digital-asset derivatives platform[108]. CZ was also forced to resign as CEO[109].

Interference in less centralized or supposedly decentralized entities is even more controversial. The Tornado Cash case is particularly illustrative: in theory, it is a decentralized protocol operating on the Ethereum blockchain. From a functional point of view, it is a Digital Law that allows users to make transactions private and anonymous[110].

Payments sent from a wallet can be traced on the blockchain because transactions are public. Contrary to what the mainstream media often suggests, many public blockchains are more transparent than traditional payment systems: once a wallet address is known, anyone can view all of its transactions.

Tornado Cash works by pooling funds together. It combines deposits from many users and then allows funds to be withdrawn in a way that breaks the direct link between deposit and withdrawal addresses. In short, the origin and destination of payments become untraceable.

From a theoretical and ideal perspective, a protocol such as Tornado Cash should be out of reach

---

[108] Jha, P. (22 November 2023). "Binance, CZ settlement with US DOJ 'bullish for Bitcoin ETF,' crypto community says", Cointelegraph.

[109] Wright, T. (21 November 2023). "US officials announce $4.3B settlement with Binance, plea deal with CZ", Cointelegraph.

[110] In earlier chapters, I referred to Monero as an example of a privacy-focused blockchain. Tornado Cash, by contrast, provides privacy on top of a transparent blockchain such as Ethereum.

of States, since it is decentralized and its code is open. But it would be a mistake to underestimate State machinery. At present, only what is 100% decentralized and has no identifiable leadership is truly difficult to attack.

Tornado Cash is, in principle, decentralized. It is not a classic company with a traditional management team. Instead, the protocol is maintained largely by its community of users and developers.

The most effective way for a State to attempt to neutralize such a protocol is to attack both its "heads" and its "tails". On the one hand, it can sanction anyone who works with or uses the protocol and block wallets associated with it, effectively freezing the crypto-assets they contain[111]. On the other hand, it can arrest visible leaders and send a chilling message to the rest of the community.

In August 2022, the U.S. Treasury Department, through the Office of Foreign Assets Control (OFAC), sanctioned Tornado Cash, arguing that it had been used to launder more than 7 billion dollars in virtual currencies since 2019[112].

---

[111] Technically, crypto-assets cannot be frozen on-chain by State order unless the protocol is explicitly designed to allow it, as in some CBDC models. In practice, however, States can freeze assets by coercing centralized intermediaries.

[112] According to the U.S. Treasury, Tornado Cash was allegedly used to launder funds linked to high-profile hacks, including operations attributed to North Korea's Lazarus Group.

Rather than sanctioning a company or an individual, OFAC sanctioned a protocol. The move was comparable to outlawing email because some criminals use it, or banning a general-purpose tool like PlayStation because certain users coordinate crimes through it.

OFAC also blocked dozens of wallets linked to the protocol. Shortly afterwards, Dutch authorities arrested Tornado Cash developer Alexey Pertsev on suspicion of money laundering through the platform. He spent nine months in prison before being released under supervision[113]. Other co-founders, such as Roman Semenov and Roman Storm, were also charged and face potential sentences of up to 20 years in prison[114].

This was a major blow to the cryptocurrency community. It is clear that whenever States identify what they regard as enemies within the Internet Jurisdiction, they will use all available tools to neutralize them.

For now, it is a kind of proxy war: in practice, only what is fully decentralized retains a strong defense. Even Bitcoin could be declared illegal by most States, although such a coordinated move currently seems unlikely.

---

[113] Jha, P. (20 April 2023). "Tornado Cash dev Alexey Pertsev set to be released from prison under surveillance, Cointelegraph.

[114] Andersen, D. (23 August 2023). "Tornado Cash co-founders charged with money laundering, sanctions violations", Cointelegraph.

However, in a landmark decision, the U.S. Fifth Circuit Court of Appeals ruled that the sanctions imposed by the Treasury Department on Tornado Cash's immutable smart contracts were unlawful.

The court held that, although OFAC has authority to act against property, Tornado Cash's open-source contracts are not "property" in the conventional sense because they are not susceptible to being owned by anyone. Many observers consider this a victory for freedom and privacy in the digital realm[115].

Finally, in March 2025, the U.S. government officially removed all sanctions on Tornado Cash and delisted it from the sanctions register[116]. Nevertheless, the episode has left a lasting mark: it shows that States are willing to test the limits of their power over decentralized technologies.

The U.S. SEC has also brought numerous enforcement actions against blockchains, exchanges, and protocols[117]. As the Internet community grows stronger and more organized, State power will gradually diminish, and pure decentralization will become less crucial. In the long run, mixed systems will coexist and, perhaps, eventually converge into a new hybrid legal order.

---

[115] Fifth Circuit Court of Appeals, decision on Tornado Cash sanctions (2024), which held that the Treasury had exceeded its authority by treating immutable smart contracts as property.

[116] U.S. Department of the Treasury (21 March 2025). "Tornado Cash Delisting", press release.

[117] The list of SEC enforcement actions related to digital-asset markets can be consulted on the Commission's official website under "Cybersecurity and Enforcement Actions".

II. Why New Technologies Are Difficult to Understand

"It will therefore be crucial that you see the world anew, looking from the outside in to reanalyze much that you have probably taken for granted."

William Rees-Mogg and James Dale Davidson, The Sovereign Individual

1. Learning by analogy to understand Bitcoin and crypto assets.

I believe that the greatest fortune of a newborn child, after coming into the world, is the ability to learn almost effortlessly. The baby's metabolism pushes him to perform reflex movements through which he acquires knowledge under a simple cause-and-effect mechanism. Within a few months, to the surprise of his parents, especially if he is their first child, he can spend hours knocking objects over again and again or listening to the sounds produced when he bangs a toy on the floor.

It is also true that toddlers learn through another very basic system, the hit-and-miss method. They fall down, stick their fingers into a socket, smear jam on the wall, or crush their fingers when a door suddenly swings shut. Unfortunately, the first learning system fades with age, while the second one does not.

Childhood is characterized by an open mind. Everything is new: smells, lights, colors, and sensations. Life is an eternal present full of surprises. A baby will not be shocked if his father suddenly appears to fly through the living room. To him, it seems just as normal as the first time he saw his father scream hysterically at the television (later he will learn this is called a goal), or the first time he watched sunbeams spill through the window or stared at colorful jets of light coming from a screen. During this stage, a child's brain is exceptionally receptive. This is why children can even learn new languages naturally and efficiently[118].

In practical terms, this means that very young children operate with almost no mental filters. They absorb patterns first and explanations later. Adults usually do the opposite. We demand a theory before we accept a new pattern.

That is why new technologies feel so foreign to many professionals: their brains insist on fitting every unknown object into a familiar box instead of allowing themselves to simply observe how it behaves.

After this early stage, another learning mechanism based on analogy develops. New concepts are understood by comparing them with ideas we already know. This is precisely the cognitive process used by most people who begin to study blockchain and crypto assets. The real difficulty at this stage is choosing the right analogy in the first place.

For example, many people instinctively associate a blockchain with a traditional company and equate tokens or crypto assets with company shares. At first glance, the comparison looks reasonable. Both seem to involve ownership and value. However, starting from that assumption sends the student down a labyrinth with a locked door at the end, and most of the time, he does not even realize it.

---

[118] Unfortunately, learning a language effortlessly only happens around the age of two.

A company is a legal entity created under the laws of a specific country. It has managers, employees, shareholders, a registered office, and accounting obligations. A public blockchain, by contrast, is a technical protocol that anyone in the world can use. It does not have a legal passport, a board of directors, or a headquarters. Confusing the two is like confusing traffic rules with the car manufacturer: one is a shared language everyone follows, the other is a private business that chooses to participate in that language.

A trading company is therefore not comparable to a blockchain. A blockchain is an open-source protocol used either to transmit value, as in the case of Bitcoin, or to create smart contracts and decentralized applications, as in the case of Ethereum. Comparing a blockchain to a company is like comparing a space rocket to an elephant, simply because both are large objects that move from one place to another.

In my view, Wikipedia is one of the best analogies for understanding what a blockchain is and how it works. Both systems are based on decentralization. In Wikipedia, anyone with internet access can edit its articles. Control of the information is not exercised by a single central authority but by the community of users who voluntarily contribute content and corrections.

Bitcoin functions in a similar way, operating on a decentralized blockchain network that is voluntarily supported by thousands of individuals and entities around the world. Transactions are confirmed by a distributed network of nodes rather than a centralized entity such as a bank or a state agency. Decentralization becomes a shield against censorship, because there is no single building, office, or server that can be shut down to stop Bitcoin within the Internet Jurisdiction.

Both Wikipedia and Bitcoin are also governed by transparency. Any change to a Wikipedia article is recorded in its edit history, showing who made the change, when, and usually why. Likewise, Bitcoin maintains a public ledger of all transactions on its blockchain, allowing anyone to verify transfers and follow the movement of bitcoins[119].

Email is probably the best everyday example for understanding what a digital currency, such as Bitcoin, is. Both are digital processes that allow the transfer of something over the internet: information in the case of email and value in the case of Bitcoin. Both use specific sender and receiver addresses, and neither requires an intermediary or central counterparty to move a message or a payment from A to B. In that sense, a digital currency is like the email of a blockchain[120].

There is, however, an important difference. Email created digital abundance: the marginal cost of

---

[119] The closest parallel to a blockchain is not a company but certain internet protocols. Blockchains, which function as decentralized protocols, are very similar, for example, to the TCP/IP protocol that enables data communication over a network without belonging to any specific entity.

[120] This idea is developed by Andreas Antonopoulos (2016) in The Internet of Money, Volume II, in the chapter "Maturing Out of Infancy." Merkle Boom LLC, Kindle edition.

sending one more message became almost zero. Bitcoin introduced the opposite idea, digital scarcity: there will only ever be 21 million bitcoins. Understanding this contrast is essential. For the first time in history, we can send something that behaves like digital cash rather than a simple copy of information.

When someone tells me that a blockchain is just another kind of company, I think of the movie Back to the Future. I imagine a character from the sixteenth century being transported to the twenty-first century and shown an airplane.

After exhausting himself searching for the missing mental link, he finally finds what he believes is the right analogy. He concludes that a ship is better because an airplane does not allow any sails to be raised.

He does not really understand what an airplane is or what it is used for, so he would never dare to board one of those flying contraptions. He lacks any prior experience that would let him compare the new invention with something from his own world. This is what happens when people begin studying blockchain technology. To understand it today, you have to make the mental effort to travel into the future.

The study of entirely new things requires new analogies. Academic degrees and professional titles earned in prestigious schools, most of them grounded in an educational model inherited from the Industrial Revolution, turn out to be insufficient for understanding this kind of technological break. Imagine a professional who wants to study Bitcoin. On paper, he seems perfectly prepared: he holds a double degree in business administration and law, an MBA in finance and investment, and has years of experience managing a listed equity fund.

He relies on this experience and knowledge to evaluate the new asset called Bitcoin. For years, he refused to listen to the so-called siren song of this strange digital currency. It is not backed by any state. It is not regulated like the instruments he knows. It is volatile.

It is supposedly useful for money laundering, and so many other stories he reads in the financial press. He gladly follows the opinions of experts, especially Bill Gates and Warren Buffett, whose photos he keeps framed in his home and office. To him, it is obvious: from a traditional technical point of view, Bitcoin is worthless.

But two events occur that push him to dig deeper. First, BlackRock decides to launch a Bitcoin exchange-traded fund. This is curious because those professionals are not exactly naïve, and neither is he. Second, his cousin, whom he always considered the least talented member of the family, suddenly buys a Lamborghini or at least posts one on social media. Years earlier, that same cousin told him that Bitcoin was the future. How can it be that the supposedly least sophisticated investor in the family has been right for so long?

He begins his painstaking research. As with all his investments, he starts with a fundamental analysis. He tries to understand Bitcoin's financial performance. He looks for data such as revenue, earnings, cash flow, and profit margins. Soon, he discovers something that makes him uncomfortable: there is no income statement, because Bitcoin is not a company.

He then looks in vain for a balance sheet. He wants to study assets, liabilities, and shareholders' equity to assess the financial health of this strange protocol. Again, the exercise makes no sense because Bitcoin is a blockchain network, not a corporation.

He also tries to calculate familiar financial ratios, dividends, and growth rates. He looks for revenue and earnings growth that might justify a valuation. He even runs his usual technical analysis, searching for price trends and indicators as if he were analyzing a stock. At the end, he applies the first sacred rule in his investment manual: never invest in what you do not understand.

At this point, he is completely lost. He cannot answer basic questions such as:

- What is the economic proposition of Bitcoin?
- When is the next Bitcoin halving?
- How many bitcoins will ultimately be issued?
- When will the last bitcoin be mined?
- Can a Bitcoin be divided into smaller units?

- Can Bitcoin become a deflationary currency in the long run?

And a more painful question that sooner or later he will have to confront: What if I am not the smartest person in the room, and my cousin is not as naïve as I thought?

He never encountered these questions during his undergraduate or graduate studies, nor in his professional experience as an investor. To truly understand Bitcoin, he would have to put aside his thick textbooks and sophisticated models and instead go to the essence of the crypto asset.

Only then would he see that Bitcoin's rules are designed so that, over time, the digital currency becomes scarcer and therefore more valuable. He would understand that it is primarily a long-term investment and that its closest historical relative is not a stock but gold, which, like Bitcoin, is neither issued nor backed by any government. For now, there is no other asset that shares all of these characteristics.

A useful exercise for any newcomer is to forget about price charts for a moment and simply answer a few key questions: Who defines Bitcoin's rules? How can those rules be changed? How many new units are created each day, and for how long? Who can censor or reverse a transaction? Clear answers to these questions reveal more about the asset than hundreds of pages of traditional financial analysis.

If our investor eventually decides to buy bitcoin and remain patient, history suggests that in ten years he might well abandon the tedious task of updating and reconciling company data day after day[121]. Bitcoin must be studied and understood with intellectual honesty. After that, the task is to invest, wait, and let time do its work.

Many experienced investors have already understood Bitcoin. Yet it is also true that the more attached someone is to his prior criteria, the less open-minded he tends to be, and the harder it becomes for him to grasp the nature of this novelty. That is the central difficulty with changes of the magnitude brought by Bitcoin and crypto assets: their similarities with the past are hard to find, and the differences are profound.

This required "open-mindedness" demands, first of all, the humility to set aside one's own judgment and partially become like a child again, allowing oneself to be surprised without constantly judging[122].

Using the wrong analogies inevitably leads to the wrong conclusions. Whoever wants to dive into the

---

[121] At least these are the historical data. However, this is not investment advice but an invitation to study in greater depth the rules contained in the Bitcoin Digital Law.

[122] This difficulty is not new. Two thousand years ago, Nicodemus struggled to understand the "good news" of the kingdom of heaven and was told that he had to be born again. Gospel of John 3:3: "Jesus answered and said unto him, Verily, verily, I say unto thee, Except a man be born again, he cannot see the kingdom of God. Nicodemus saith unto him, How can a man be born when he is old? Can he enter the second time into his mother's womb, and be born? Jesus answered, Verily, verily, I say unto thee, Except a man be born of water and of the Spirit, he cannot enter into the kingdom of God. That which is born of the flesh is flesh; and that which is born of the Spirit is spirit."

pool of new technologies must accept that there is no life jacket made of past experience. He must learn how to swim again, away from stagnant and overregulated waters, to reach a new, freer, and more decentralized ocean.

Closed-mindedness affects both individuals and states. If we dust off the history of some of the most anti-innovative laws ever enacted, we find examples as striking as the so-called "Red Flag Act," passed in the United Kingdom in 1865[123]. This regulation imposed severe restrictions on early motor vehicles. Officially, the first priority was the safety of citizens. Safety, especially "consumer safety," is very fashionable again in the West.

The Red Flag Act required every motor vehicle to travel with a crew of three, which made the technology almost impractical: a driver, an engineer to keep the machine running, and a person walking in front carrying a red flag to warn pedestrians and horse-drawn carriages.

If the United Kingdom had bet decisively on innovation in the automotive industry, the nineteenth century might have ended with debates about spark plugs, headlights, or steering systems. Instead, one of the country's great urban concerns was horse manure.

As The Times reported in 1894, "In 50 years, all the streets of London will be buried under three meters of

---

[123] Officially, it was called the "Locomotive Act."

dung"[124]. Following that line of thinking, will we end the twenty-first century in the West arguing about the recycling of our own waste while ignoring much larger technological questions?

Innovation blindness can even affect entrepreneurs who once changed the world but later lost the ability to see the future. At different times, respected figures have argued that the iPod would be a failure, that we would never have a computer in every home, that vacuum cleaners would be powered by nuclear energy, that television had no future, or that airplanes could never carry more than ten passengers[125]. History proved all of them wrong.

New markets are often reserved for small, agile pioneers. Many incumbents, companies, institutions, and even states have the size of giants but the reflexes of dinosaurs. They struggle to adapt to the technological meteorite that is already reshaping the planet.

Taxi drivers kept renewing their expensive taxi licenses and arguing with one another at taxi stands while Uber quietly transformed urban transport. Hotels focused on buying new properties in tourist areas while they failed to detect the rise of Airbnb's new lodging

---

[124] Ansede, M. (November 14, 2018). "La gran crisis de las boñigas de caballo de 1894 y el futuro de la humanidad." El País. Retrieved March 26, 2024, from https://elpais.com/elpais/2018/11/13/ciencia/1542126469_433670.html

[125] Minuto uno. (12 de diciembre de 2008). ¡Decilo ahora! Las diez 'profecías' tecno que nunca se cumplieron. Accessed March 22, 2024 from https://www.minutouno.com/tecno/decilo-ahora-lasdiez-profecias-quenunca-se-cumplieron-n97572

model. The yellow pages, once present in every household, vanished, while others created a Google-style internet search system[126].

Bitcoin and the broader world of crypto assets belong to that same family of disruptive innovations. They look small and exotic at first, but they quietly rewrite the rules of value, ownership, and coordination. Those who wait for every doubt to be resolved before engaging will likely arrive when the opportunity has already matured, just in time to pay the highest price for the least upside.

---

[126] These examples have been repeated so often that some are now part of business folklore, but they still serve as a reminder that even brilliant minds often underestimate technologies that do not fit their existing mental models.

2. Looks can be deceiving: Bitcoin is not what it seems, and neither are central banks.

Another problem when studying cryptoassets is that media headlines, intellectuals, and experts are biased and self-serving. They tend to emphasize and repeat that Bitcoin is volatile, unlike fiat money, which is considered stable. Likewise, cryptoasset enthusiasts, as idealistic as they are, are exposed to risky investments, sell the emergence of a new decentralized system that will do away with many modern problems. As they repeat these ideas, market abuses and other undesirable behaviors continue to surface.

Who should we believe? At first glance, the argument about volatility and its risks seems unanswerable. But if Bitcoin is analyzed from the point of view of its economic policy, we see that Bitcoin is stable and that what is not stable are the policies of the central banks. Bitcoin's deflationary system cannot be manipulated by any central entity. By contrast, central bank policies change according to criteria that are absolutely unknown to most people.

Behind the daily and weekly price swings is a very different reality. Bitcoin can fluctuate widely in the short term, especially when news events or speculation move the market, yet the rules that govern its supply are fixed in advance and known by everyone. Fiat currencies can look calm on a price chart while their purchasing power slowly erodes year after year. In other words, Bitcoin's price is volatile, but its monetary policy is not, whereas with fiat money the opposite tends to happen.

Central banks repeat ad nauseam that Bitcoin is highly volatile. They intentionally omit that Bitcoin is deflationary and that it is regulated so that its value should increase over time. To date, anyone who has invested in Bitcoin over the long term has only made a profit[127].

One of Bitcoin's mechanisms for increasing value is called "halving," and it occurs approximately every four years. We can understand it with a very basic example. Bitcoin is like a bear that hibernates, but only once every four years. In each halving, there is usually a sharp rise in Bitcoin's value, followed by a reversal and a correction.

The correction is a large drop in the Bitcoin price in what is called the "crypto winter." So far, the Bitcoin price has always exceeded the level reached in the previous halving. This is the rule: the Bitcoin value at the beginning of a halving has always been far above the value at the beginning of the previous halving.

This pattern is not magic. When the reward for miners is reduced, the new supply that enters the market is cut in half, while demand can stay the same

---

[127] Long term means at least one halving cycle to the next and, even better, a minimum investment horizon of ten years. However, this is not investment advice. Each person must make his or her own decisions.

or grow. If demand holds or increases while the flow of new coins slows down, basic economic logic suggests upward pressure on price over time. Markets are complex, and there is never a guarantee, but the protocol itself constantly moves Bitcoin in a more scarce direction.

Bitcoin is a digital currency payment system called "Bitcoin." Every ten minutes, the transactions made on the network are stored in a block that is closed by a consensus mechanism called Proof of Work (PoW). In other words, miners compete with each other to solve an equation and receive a reward in return. Every 210,000 blocks that are closed, Bitcoin rewards are cut in half. This effect is called "halving."

Unlike fiat money, whose issuance is unlimited, Bitcoin generates fewer units every four years until the year 2140, when it will stop issuing new digital assets. In other words, the last halving will take place in the year 2140.

The rewards for miners in 2009, when Bitcoin was born, were 50 Bitcoins per block. On November 28, 2012, the first halving took place, and the Bitcoin payout dropped to 25 Bitcoins per generated block. The approximate price of Bitcoin at the beginning of that halving was $12.35.

As a result of the halving effect, miners themselves will try to push up the price of Bitcoin so that it acquires more value. On July 9, 2016, the second halving took place with an approximate price of $650.63 per Bitcoin.

From this date, the miners started to receive 12.50 Bitcoins.

At the time of the third Bitcoin halving, on May 11, 2020, the approximate Bitcoin price was $8,821.63 USD[128]. As a result of the halving, miners started receiving 6.25 Bitcoin per block.

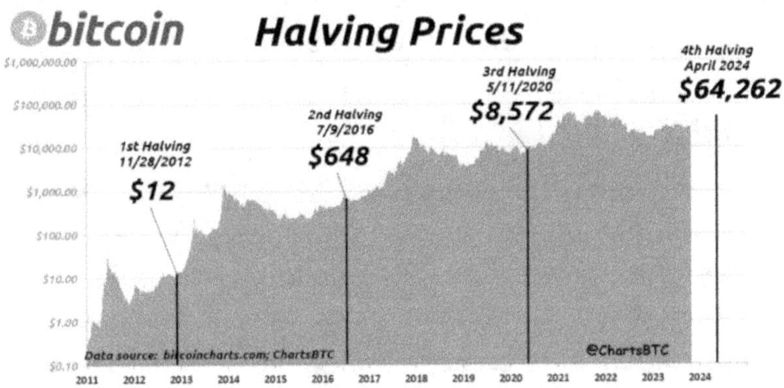

Fig 6.

The fourth halving took place on April 20, 2024, with Bitcoin valued at approximately $64,262 USD

Since that date, miners have been paid 3.125 Bitcoin per block.

In all halvings, the Bitcoin price has exceeded its level at the previous halving. The advantage of this deflationary system can be glimpsed with an example. Let us imagine that someone bought, like Tom from

---

[128] These prices are estimates based on averages for the days around each halving event and may vary slightly depending on the source of the data.

chapter 1, 83 Bitcoins with about $1,000 in 2012, before the first halving. Right now, assuming each Bitcoin is worth $75,000, those 83 Bitcoins would be valued at about $6,225,000. This is the calculation that Dick, from chapter 1, makes.

Halving has been the subject of study by many people. One of the best strategies I have read is this: buy Bitcoin 500 days before the next halving, which will be around March 2028, and sell 500 days after. This is not investment advice, so I simply encourage you to study it[129].

Even if past halving cycles have rewarded patient investors, no future cycle is guaranteed to behave in exactly the same way. Regulation, global liquidity, adoption of Bitcoin by institutions, and the behavior of other digital assets can all change how each new cycle unfolds. Anyone who wants to act on these patterns needs to understand that they are studying history, not a promise, and must manage risk accordingly.

Those who do not know how Bitcoin works, like the aforementioned stock expert, tend to think that this kind of stratospheric profit only occurred at the beginning of the Bitcoin era, back in 2009. Many believe that it is now too late. But nothing could be further from the truth. This is well known to the apparently dumb cousin. We are only at the beginning of the new digital currency. There are still 28 halvings to go until the last

---

[129] For example, one web page that describes this strategy in more detail is: https://coinedition.com/crypto-analyst-reveals-simple-bitcoin-trading-strategy-based-on-halving-events/

one in the year 2140. That is 28 times, every four years, that, if everything continues as it has so far, Bitcoin will be worth more than in the previous halving.

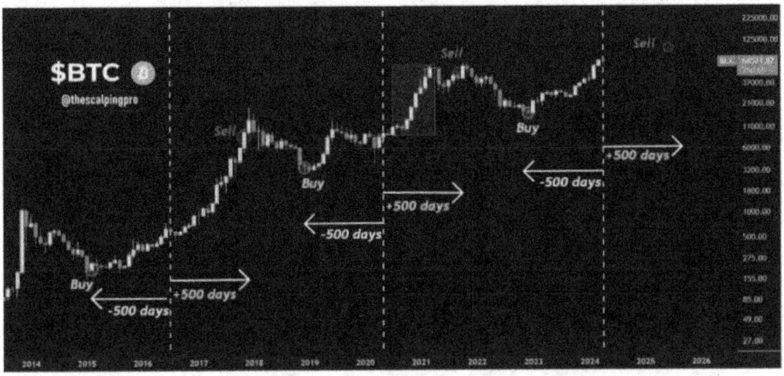

Fig. 7: Historical graph of the value of Bitcoin.
Source: @thescalpingpro [130]

I do not know what the world will be like in 2140. I do not know if it will be full of intelligent machines or if we will all speak Mandarin. What I do know is that some people will look with pride at the picture of their grandfather resting in the living room of their manor house above the fireplace. They will raise a glass in honor of that intelligent ancestor who invested in a digital asset that he barely consumed and reserved for his descendants, who are now enjoying it.

---

[130] Graph adapted from the account @thescalpingpro on X (formerly Twitter): https://x.com/thescalpingpro/status/1776315935592529939

Others, on the other hand, will think that their ancestors were clumsy, even though they had university degrees and two master's degrees[131].

Another good piece of news about Bitcoin is that its deflationary system cannot be modified or manipulated by anyone. This is the exact opposite of central bank policies. Those policies can be as capricious and changeable as the mood of a small child in front of a knick-knack store that he is not allowed to enter.

If the profession of "economic psychiatrists" existed and they worked in private, non-subsidized hospitals, they would undoubtedly diagnose the central banks, in view of the history of their changing policies, with severe bipolar economic disorder and, in some cases, with narcissistic and maniacal traits[132].

The abrupt changes in rate increases and decreases, often without prior warning, have dire consequences, first for the banks themselves. Secondly, they affect the rest of the population, who already do enough by trying to spend prudently in an environment where their money is worth less every day. Anyone who studies Bitcoin discovers this trap

---

[131] This example assumes that everything has gone well. Many inheritances, unfortunately, end in fratricidal conflict. It is a pity.

[132] Caballero, M., Ramió, A. and Carrera, M. (2020). Finanzas descentralizadas para inquietos. Cómo blockchain y las DeFi cambiaron el sistema financiero para siempre. Editorial Bubok Publishing, chapter 4, section 5 (Kindle edition). These authors point out that the pound sterling, with more than three centuries of history, has lost around 99.5 percent of its value.

and understands that what really changes, ultimately, are the policies of the central banks.

Upper limit of the U.S. federal funds target rate range*

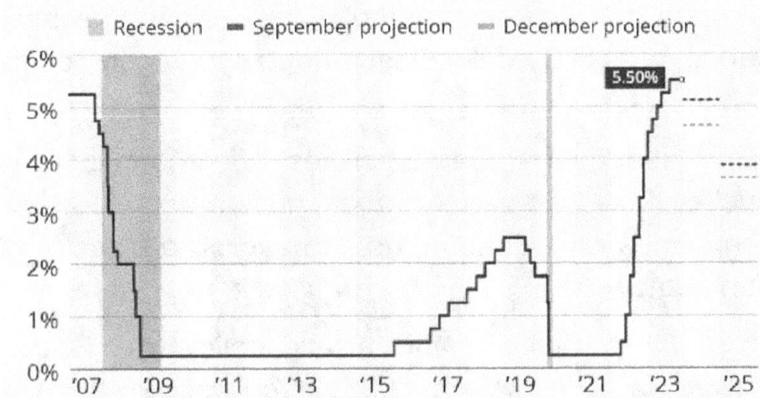

*Dotted lines indicate median projections of the midpoint of the appropriate target rate range at the end of the specif calendar year.

Source: U.S. Federal Reserve

Fig. 8.

This is a graph of the volatile rise and fall of interest rates, which only a few people, with their crystal ball plugged in, can predict. Bitcoin's economic policy cannot be changed. It is more stable than the resting pulse of a professional cyclist.

The only thing central banks are stable in is the devaluation of their own currencies. The best fiat currency in history, the pound, has devalued by approximately 99.5 percent since its creation[133].

In the postwar era, the best national currency, the German mark, lost about 71 percent of its value from January 1, 1949, to the end of June 1995. In the same period, the U.S. dollar lost about 84 percent of its value[134].

These central bank policies affect banks in a nuclear way, because banks must adapt to them, sometimes without being able to avoid the disaster of bankruptcy.

A close victim of this erratic policy was Silicon Valley Bank. In March 2023, it collapsed after the abrupt rate hike produced by the Federal Reserve, which began in March 2022 to combat inflation that the central bank itself had helped to generate[135].

---

[133] Davison, J. D. and Rees-Mogg, W. (2022). The Sovereign Individual: Mastering the Transition to the Information Age. Bubok Publishing (Madrid), Kindle edition.

[134] Eberly, J. C., Kalemli-Özcan, Ş., Gourinchas, P.-O., Steinsson, J., and Filiz Unsal, F. (November 9, 2023). "How have Fed interest rate hikes affected other national economies?" Brookings Institution. Accessed March 2024 from https://www.brookings.edu/articles/how-have-fed-interest-rate-hikes-affected-other-national-economies/

[135] There is no free money, and whoever promises it is not telling the truth, because the only one who can give for free is God. In Christian theology, God is love. A central bank is not God. From the start of the pandemic in March 2020 to the end of 2021, the Federal Reserve's balance sheet expanded from approximately 4 trillion dollars to about 8.8 trillion dollars. This increase largely reflects the creation of new money to buy financial assets. In addition, the U.S. Congress passed several stimulus packages, including the CARES Act in March 2020 (2.2 trillion dollars), the Coronavirus Relief and Response Supplemental Appropriations Act in December 2020 (900 billion dollars), and the American Rescue Plan in March 2021 (1.9 trillion dollars). Inflation is therefore not like the law of gravity, which happens naturally.

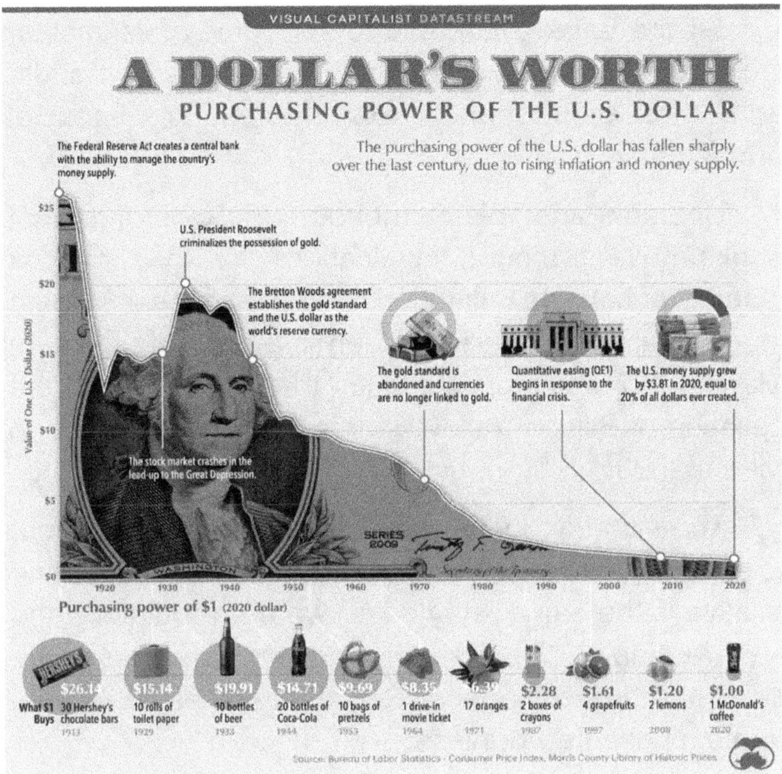

Fig. 9: Purchasing value of the dollar from 1920 to 2020.

This change in monetary policy had several effects on financial markets and banking institutions. For example, the market value of long-term bonds decreased as new bonds were issued at higher interest rates in line with the Fed's rate hikes.

Many investors requested withdrawals from older bonds with lower yields compared with the new bonds that offered higher yields. Silicon Valley Bank, like many other institutions, held significant investments in long-term bonds that lost value because of these rate increases. Banks then faced liquidity pressures.

Silicon Valley Bank had to sell some of its assets, including bonds, at a loss to meet withdrawal demands, and that sale further exacerbated its financial problems.

Unstable and volatile monetary policies of central banks have profound implications for the financial stability of banking institutions and the financial system in general. The Fed's sudden interest rate hike in March 2022 was a critical factor that contributed to the collapse of Silicon Valley Bank and Signature Bank in March 2023.

The situation looks like a time bomb that is about to explode. However, the message they keep repeating is always the same: stay calm, we are regulated, and we are stable. At the same time, they warn us to be careful with Bitcoin, because it is unregulated, volatile, and supposedly worthless.

Rising rates also make it more difficult to repay mortgage loans, which affects the real estate sector and, once again, citizens and banks. In June 2024, the investment company Pimco warned of new bank failures derived from the real estate crisis caused by rate hikes. Specifically, it said that it foresees more regional bank failures in the United States due to a very high concentration of distressed commercial real estate loans on their books[136].

[136] Benítez, L. (June 11, 2024). "Crisis inmobiliaria provocará más quiebras de bancos regionales en EE. UU., advierte Pimco." Infobae. Accessed August 14, 2024, from https://www.infobae.com/america/agencias/2024/06/11/crisis-

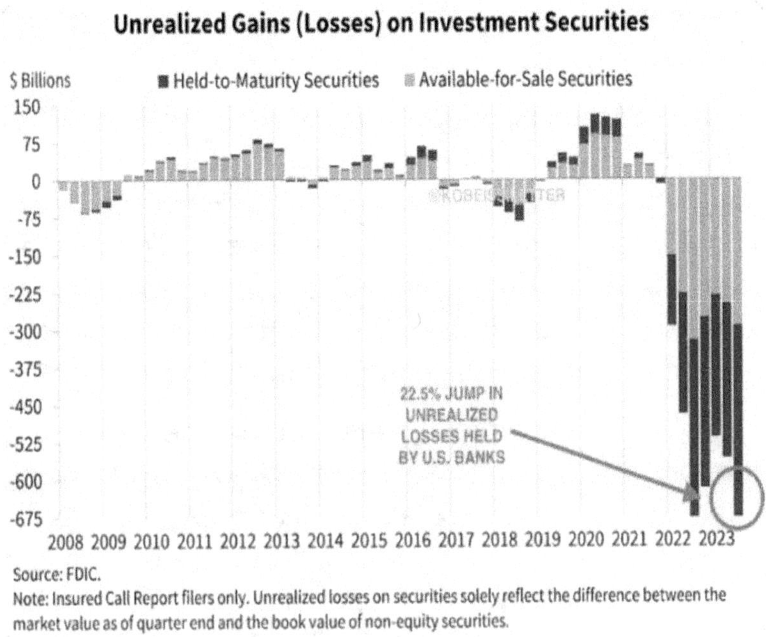

Fig. 10: Graph of unrealized losses in U.S. banking, with 2023 data showing approximately 575 billion U.S. dollars[137]

The case of Silicon Valley Bank is a clear example of the weakness of the changing financial system. A few months earlier, in November 2022, the cryptoasset exchange FTX collapsed. Faced with this collapse, criticism from the traditional system, such as central banks, immediately appeared with the usual

inmobiliaria-provocara-mas-quiebras-de-bancos-regionales-en-eeuu-advierte-pimco/

[137] Kochkodin, B. (May 31, 2023). "Banks' 515 Billion Dollars of Quarterly Paper Losses Is Actually an Improvement." Forbes. Accessed October 5, 2024, from https://www.forbes.com/sites/brandonkochkodin/2023/05/31/banks-515-billion-of-quarterly-paper-losses-is-actually-an-improvement/

arguments, claiming that these entities were not regulated and were not backed by the state.

In this financial quicksand, a curious case was that of the cryptoasset company Circle. It was not affected, at least not directly, by the fall of FTX. However, it was fully affected by the fall of the regulated Silicon Valley Bank, where it held about $3.3 billion to guarantee its stablecoin USDC, which is the stablecoin referred to in chapter 1 when discussing the Tether Digital Law[138].

Following the warnings of the referenced entities is therefore no guarantee of success. Not using cryptoassets on an exchange like FTX but having money in a bank like Silicon Valley Bank was not exactly a guarantee for Circle either. Silicon Valley Bank was indeed bailed out, unlike the FTX exchange, but the cost of that rescue for citizens was about 20 billion U.S. dollars[139].

The security offered by Bitcoin is that its financial policy cannot vary. It is a law as immovable as the law of gravity. In contrast, the policies of central banks are absolutely variable, with drastic rises and falls in rates.

With the law of gravity of the central banks, one day you can be glued to the ground, and the next day

---

[138] Ehret, T. (March 15, 2023). "5 Important Regulatory Aspects of the Silicon Valley Bank Collapse." Thomson Reuters. Accessed March 22, 2024, from https://www.thomsonreuters.com/en-us/posts/corporates/regulatory-aspects-svb-collapse/

[139] Jiménez, M. (March 22, 2023). "El rescate de Silicon Valley Bank deja un agujero de 20.000 millones de dólares." El País. Accessed March 26, 2024, from https://elpais.com/economia/2023-03-27/el-rescate-de-silicon-valley-bank-deja-un-agujero-de-20000-millones-de-dolares.html

you can be floating in the air. Unfortunately, the whole economy has to adapt to these gravitational changes in the policies of central banks, like a circus juggler, with the real danger that a crash can be devastating[140].

[140] For further study of the effects of government manipulation on the economy, I recommend reading chapter 6 "The Information System of Capitalism" from the book "The Bitcoin Standard" by Saifedean Ammous.

3. Elites do not want you to understand Bitcoin.

Technological innovation is what makes human societies prosperous. As I pointed out in Chapter 1, the fundamental driver of human progress is technological solutions to problems[141]. But achieving them is not always straightforward. They usually involve replacing old structures with new ones. The internet, crypto assets, and artificial intelligence are digital tectonic plates that, like an earthquake, are reshaping the world from top to bottom.

The opposition to progress we see today is, unfortunately, commonplace in human history. There are numerous examples. The Soviet communist system generated very weak economic incentives among its population to invent and progress. Its power structure was so destructive and pernicious that innovation became as inaccessible a luxury as caviar.

Survival was paramount. Nevertheless, and in spite of everything, the USSR made great strides in the military and aerospace fields. After millions suffered starvation, executions, and forced labor in concentration camps, the USSR was able to launch the

---

[141] Kremer, M. (1993). Population growth and technological change: one million B.C. to 1990. The Quarterly Journal of Economics, 108(3), 681–716.

first dog and the first person into space. They also came up with the infamous AK-47 assault rifle[142].

A country that does not innovate will sooner or later be relegated to poverty. Another illustrative example was the Ottoman Empire, so powerful in the 16th century. The striking fact is that in 1800, only 2% of the Empire's inhabitants could read and write. In contrast, in England, it was 60% for adult men and 40% for adult women[143].

We could blame this on religion, climate, or geography. But the origin of this deficient situation was the unwillingness of elites and rulers to facilitate the technologies of their time. Specifically, Muslims were prohibited from printing in Arabic. This was decreed in 1485 by the Sultan of the Empire, Bayezid II. This criterion was later ratified by Sultan Selim I in 1515. The first printing press was permitted in Ottoman lands in 1727[144]. In Egypt, the first printing press was set up in 1798 by the French[145].

The consequence of a country, an empire, or a nation refusing to innovate can be devastating for its population. This is the challenge we face today more than ever, with the new technologies emanating from the internet.

---

[142] Acemoglu, D., and Robinson, J. A. (2012). Why Nations Fail (ch. 7, "The Turning Point"). Deusto: Kindle edition.

[143] Idem.

[144] Idem.

[145] Idem.

Even if the power of modern elites is wavering, our responsibility is to maintain an active attitude, keep an open mind, and offer resistance to the official current of thought. It is no coincidence that criticism against Bitcoin, cryptocurrencies, and artificial intelligence is regularly spread. They do not want us to understand and employ these new technologies outside of their control.

And I say official current of thought because it is not improvised. It is carefully prepared and directed. These messages are repeated over and over again from various tribunes, both by the media and by politicians, rulers, and tycoons. We are told that Bitcoin is not real, when technically it is similar to electronic money.

They repeat that it is dangerous because it is not regulated by them, when in fact it is self-regulated and deployed in the internet jurisdiction. They warn us that it is volatile, that it is used for trafficking, that it is environmentally unfriendly, and so on.

One of the simplest ways to spot narrative engineering is to ask a basic question: What is being emphasized, and what is being quietly omitted?

With Bitcoin, the official narrative emphasizes short term price swings while minimizing the system's long term design, including its supply schedule and the incentives that make the network resilient.

In practice, the messaging tends to follow three predictable moves. First, the innovation is framed as reckless or immoral. Second, the public is told to wait for official permission. Third, once institutions can tax it, monitor it, or monetize it, they adopt the same technology on their own terms.

Many frightened citizens follow the paternalistic state's guidelines. They shy away from Bitcoin and crypto assets until the powers that be raise the red flag and later give the green light to new technologies. It will be then that the naive citizen will acquire, not Bitcoin, but the official crypto asset of the state, called a CBDC. Of course, he may be unaware that it is like having a snake in the house. He may be unaware that any payment he makes with this money can be controlled.

In contrast to open networks, a CBDC can be designed so that payments are traceable by default and money becomes programmable in ways cash never was. A government can attach conditions to spending, restrict where funds may be used, freeze balances, or apply negative interest rates by policy. That does not make a CBDC inevitable, but it does clarify why monetary control and surveillance are central concerns in this debate.

For further study of the effects of government manipulation on the economy, I recommend chapter 6, "The Information System of Capitalism," from the book The Bitcoin Standard, by Saifedean Ammous[146].

[146] For further study of the effects of government manipulation on the economy, I recommend reading chapter 6, "The Information System of Capitalism", from the book "The Bitcoin Standard", by Saifedean Ammous.

Every now and then, the mainstream media, through a motivated bureaucrat or an official intellectual of a central bank, repeats the same clichés. For example, Ulrich Bindseil and Jürgen Schaaf published on February 22, 2024, on the blog of the European Central Bank (ECB)[147] that Bitcoin has not fulfilled its promise to become a decentralized global digital currency.

They also highlighted that it is used for illegitimate transactions, that it does not fulfill the investment function, and that it is not a means of payment due to its conceptual design and technological limitations. They also criticized that Bitcoin transactions are cumbersome, slow, and expensive. Finally, they stressed that its value is highly volatile and unsuitable for payments.

Evidently, the report ignores Bitcoin's halving mechanism, whereby Bitcoin's value tends to rise over the long term. They also fail to report that only 21 million units will ever be issued, and that both the halving and the issuance limit make Bitcoin a deflationary currency, unlike the money issued by the European Central Bank.

This proposal is, at least for the moment, a monetary alternative for people trying to hedge against inflation. Nor do they report that Bitcoin is one of the

---

[147] Bindseil, U., and Schaaf, J. (February 22, 2024). ETF approval for Bitcoin: the naked emperor's new clothes. The ECB Blog. Accessed April 3, 2024, from https://www.ecb.europa.eu/press/blog/date/2024/html/ecb.blog20240222~0929f86e23.en.html

strongest payment systems in the world in terms of resilience, because it is difficult to attack due to the number of nodes that support it.

And this happens precisely because it is decentralized. They criticize that it is not completely decentralized, when they are the ones who exercise the centralization of money.

Of course, they do not mention Bitcoin's profitability. It is more profitable than gold. Gold, from 1970 to 2020, went from $35 to more than $1,900 per ounce. That is an increase of approximately 5,400%. Bitcoin, from 2010, when it began to have significant value, to 2024, has gone from fractions of a penny to about $69,000. That is an increase of millions of percent.

These subsidized minions also often fail to mention that fiat money is not supported by gold, and that they print unlimited banknotes, which is not the case with Bitcoin. A bit of serious soul searching would reveal that the euro, the great currency of Europe, has devalued by 85% compared to gold since its inception, based on 2020 data[148].

They do not recognize, nor will they ever say, that in terms of profitability, since the beginning of the decade, Bitcoin is considered the best performing

---

[148] Martínez Gallego, J. M. (April 30, 2020). Desde su creación hace 20 años, el euro se ha devaluado un 85% frente al oro. Oro Información. Accessed May 21, 2024, from https://oroinformacion.com/desde-su-creacion-hace-20-anos-el-euro-se-ha-devaluado-en-un-85-frente-al-oro/

asset, light years ahead of the second, with a return of 60,000,000%. In second place, Netflix, at 3,700%[149].

A central bank criticizing Bitcoin technology is like a letter carrier ranting because email is not supported on paper. The financial system has taken years to evolve, as it had little need to innovate due to its monopoly status. International bank payments can take days and sometimes longer.

This does not happen with crypto assets because their technology can settle value faster. Regarding the use of crypto assets for illegal payments, they do not report that both the euro and the dollar have been common currencies for money laundering.

Finally, they also fail to point out that banking is a luxury good not accessible to all: one third of the world's population is not allowed to access banking[150]. Bitcoin and other cryptocurrencies do not exclude anyone and can help solve the problem of access to payment systems.

Access matters because payment rails are not just a convenience. They are a gatekeeping mechanism that determines who can save, who can transact, and who can participate in digital commerce. Open

---

[149] Caballero, M., Ramió, A., and Carrera, M. (2020). Finanzas descentralizadas para inquietos: Cómo Blockchain y las DeFi cambiaron el sistema financiero para siempre. Editorial Bubok Publishing (chapter 4): Kindle edition.

[150] Semana. (March 24, 2016). Cerca del 30% de la población mundial no posee una cuenta bancaria. Accessed November 1, 2023, from https://www.semana.com/economia/articulo/cuantas-personas-en-el-mundo-tienen-acceso-al-sistema-financiero/221680/

networks reduce gatekeeping by allowing anyone with a basic device and connectivity to hold value and send it.

Another example of official messaging is the Bank of England. Jon Cunliffe, who was Deputy Governor for Financial Stability of the entity, stressed, in accordance with his position, the danger of cryptocurrencies for financial stability[151]. He pointed out that they are unsupported and volatile. Volatility is an oft-repeated criticism by official propaganda. As we have pointed out before, the motive is to prevent us from focusing on what matters, which is not the price, but Bitcoin's stable, deflationary economic policy.

It happens in the United States as well. Chapter 8 of the March 2023 Economic Report of the President[152] repeats the same arguments, the same criticisms, and the same omissions.

Not only central banks, but also famous tycoons have criticized crypto assets. Among these, Bill Gates and Warren Buffett stand out. They are smart, successful, and wealthy entrepreneurs. Their opinions are followed by millions of people.

Bill Gates has stated that cryptocurrencies are causing deaths and that they are only good for buying

---

[151] Cunliffe, J. (October 13, 2021). Is "crypto" a financial stability risk? Bank of England. Accessed April 4, 2024, from https://www.bankofengland.co.uk/speech/2021/october/jon-cunliffe-swifts-sibos-2021

[152] The report can be downloaded here: https://www.whitehouse.gov/wp-content/uploads/2023/03/ERP-2023.pdf

drugs[153]. One thing is clear: cryptocurrencies have not killed anyone. The only technology designed to kill is military technology, about which Mr. Gates has said nothing. Some technologies are involved in deaths every year, including traffic, air, railway, or maritime accidents. On these, there is no record of any saving action by Bill Gates. Cryptocurrencies' killing seems more like a good plot for a Tarantino movie than a serious assessment.

The subject of drugs and crypto assets is also frequently used by official propaganda. I have already cited the European Central Bank report of February 22, 2024, that highlighted illegitimate Bitcoin payments. Of course, Bill Gates was no exception. Drug traffickers historically have not used Bitcoin but dollars in their dealings. In 2015, in Colombia, a farmer named Jose Mariena Cartolos found $600 million buried, not bitcoins, but dollars, that belonged to Pablo Escobar[154]. The farmer received a donation from his country's government to start a palm plantation on land that belonged to his family. To date, neither Bill Gates nor any moral bureaucrat has asked the U.S. government to withdraw the dollar for being used by drug traffickers in their illegal businesses.

---

[153] BBC. (March 1, 2018). Bill Gates says cryptocurrencies cause deaths. Accessed April 4, 2024, from https://www.bbc.com/news/technology-43239781

[154] Uno Santa Fe. (November 13, 2015). Un campesino colombiano encontró enterrada parte de la fortuna de Pablo Escobar. Accessed October 23, 2023, from https://www.unosantafe.com.ar/un-campesino-colombiano-encontro-enterrada-parte-la-fortuna-que-era-pablo-escobar-n2069518.html

Those who really launder money, and that Bill Gates and the official mainstream of thought purposefully omit, are the banks themselves and other legal structures created for the purpose. Only a legal entity can make use of the magic wand by virtue of which "B assets," non-legal, are transformed into "A assets," legal tender. Assets B can be crypto assets, dollars, euros, or any legal tender.

Nordea Bank, headquartered in Helsinki, has been indicted for laundering €3.5 billion of Russian money[155]. However, the bank that takes the top prize is Danske, which, through its Estonian branch, laundered a whopping $230 billion[156].

New revelations from an investigation by BuzzFeed and the International Consortium of Investigative Journalists have shed light on the extent to which the world's largest banks have been complicit in international money laundering. Their million-dollar racketeering took place during the years 1999 and 2017. Believe it or not, before 2009, and despite the fact that cryptocurrencies did not exist, banks were laundering money.

---

[155] Vadala, F. (July 10, 2024). El mayor banco escandinavo, acusado de blanquear 3.500 millones de euros de dinero ruso. Decripto.org. Accessed August 16, 2024, from https://decripto.org/es/el-mayor-banco-escandinavo-acusado-de-blanquear-3-500-millones-de-euros-de-dinero-ruso/

[156] ACFCS. (September 5, 2019). Estonia, en el epicentro de los escándalos de lavado de dinero de la UE, clasifica como el país con menos probabilidades de lavar dinero según índice ALD de Basilea. delitosfinancieros.org. Accessed August 16, 2024, from https://www.delitosfinancieros.org/estonia-en-el-epicentro-de-los-escandalos-de-lavado-de-dinero-de-la-ue-clasifica-como-el-pais-con-menos-probabilidades-de-lavar-dinero-segun-indice-ald-de-basilea/

Deutsche Bank reported to authorities that it had processed suspicious payments worth $1.3 billion (€1.103 billion). JPMorgan reported suspicious transactions worth $514 billion (€436.281 billion). Standard Chartered processed $166 billion (€140.9 billion). Bank of New York Mellon, with $64 billion (€54.532 billion). Barclays, with $21.7 billion (€18.416 billion). Société Générale, with $8.5 billion (€7.213 billion). HSBC, with $4.5 billion (€3.819 billion), and Commerzbank, with $1.7 billion (€1.442 billion)[157].

A highly recommended book for understanding how legal structures are set up in order to launder capital is *Treasure Islands* by Nicholas Shaxson. This book, published in 2011, addresses the global financial system and tax havens.

The author exposes how both tax havens and offshore banking allow global corporations and the wealthy to hide huge amounts of money in order to evade taxes and regulations. Shaxson argues that territories such as the Cayman Islands, Switzerland, and the Channel Islands play a central role in the global economy, facilitating corruption, money laundering, and economic inequality.

The book also shows how governments such as the United Kingdom and the United States play a role in facilitating this opaque financial system. Shaxson

---

[157] De la Cruz, S. (September 21, 2020). Así blanqueaban cientos de miles de millones los grandes bancos mundiales. La Razón. Accessed August 16, 2024, from https://www.larazon.es/economia/20200921/tvz3rzwcy5hwdo7a62s26sdlqa.html

argues that this system contributes to growing global inequality, undermines democracies, and creates serious economic problems for countries that are unable to collect the taxes needed to fund public services.

Another criticism of Bill Gates is that cryptocurrencies in the long run are very risky[158]. In the case of Bitcoin, that argument is flatly incorrect. According to historical performance data, Bitcoin, as I have pointed out before, is the most profitable asset of the century, with returns ten times higher than the Nasdaq 100[159]. This index captures the top 100 technology companies in the United States, something that investor Gates knows perfectly well. It seems that Mr. Gates is very keen that we do not discover the secret of Bitcoin, namely that it is deflationary and not manipulable.

Bill Gates has also claimed that Bitcoin is only for the rich[160]. According to this theory, Bitcoin is merely an exclusive digital gimmick for wealthy elites to which he belongs. Just as they can spend a year in Ibiza or

---

158 Martin, E. (February 27, 2018). Bill Gates: Cryptocurrency is "super risky" over the long term. CNBC. Accessed October 23, 2023, from https://www.cnbc.com/2018/02/27/bill-gates-calls-cryptocurrency-super-risky-in-reddit-ama.html

159 Sriram, S. (March 16, 2021). Bitcoin becomes best performing asset of the decade, returning ten times more than the Nasdaq 100. Yahoo Finance. Accessed April 4, 2024, from https://finance.yahoo.com/news/bitcoin-becomes-best-performing-asset-132208120.html

160 Clarín. (February 24, 2021). Bill Gates cree que el Bitcoin es para ricos: "Si tenés menos dinero que Elon Musk, deberías tener cuidado". Accessed April 4, 2024, from https://www.clarin.com/tecnologia/bill-gates-cree-bitcoin-ricos-tenes-dinero-elon-musk-deberias-tener-cuidado-_0_CgnXSdEH-.html

skiing in the Alps, they buy Bitcoin. According to these statements, it would be logical that Bitcoin holders would be nationals of the richest countries in the world, with the highest GDP per capita, such as Luxembourg, Norway, Ireland, Switzerland, or Qatar[161].

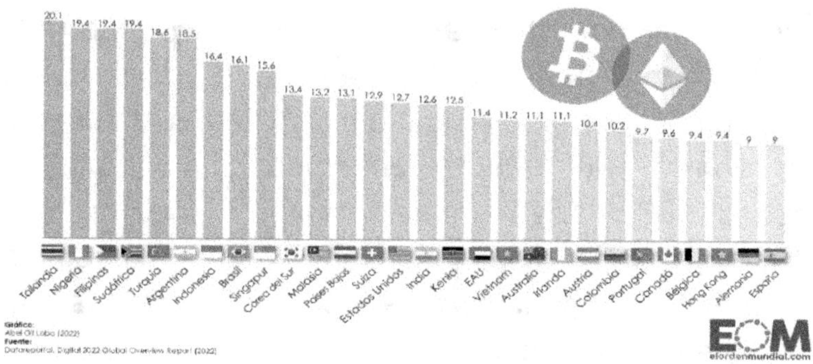

Fig. 11: % of internet users (16-64 years old) owning cryptocurrencies (2021).

But the reality is different. Figure 11 shows the percentage of internet users aged 16 to 64 owning cryptocurrencies (2021).

The countries where crypto assets are most successful include Thailand, Nigeria, the Philippines, South Africa, and Turkey, according to 2022 data[162].

The reason is simple: in countries with more inflation, citizens are looking for a way out, which the

---

[161] Fernández, R. (n.d.). Ranking de los 20 países con el mayor producto interior bruto (PIB) per cápita en 2022. Statista. Accessed October 24, 2023, from https://es.statista.com/estadisticas/600552/los-paises-con-el-mayor-producto-interior-bruto-pib-per-capita/

[162] Gil, A. (August 2, 2022). Hey cryptobro!! ¿De dónde eres? El Orden Mundial. Accessed October 4, 2024, from https://elordenmundial.com/mapas-y-graficos/paises-propietarios-criptomonedas-mundo/

state not only does not give them, but often prevents them from using, namely, cryptocurrencies.

The case that best exemplifies this process is Nigeria, where cryptocurrencies were officially banned in 2021. Despite this, their use continued to increase among its inhabitants[163]. Nigeria's crypto transaction volume grew by 9% year on year to $56.7 billion between July 2022 and June 2023[164]. Nigerians did not simply swap the casino for crypto assets. They wanted to survive inflation and the severe devaluation of their national currency, the naira.

That is why the Nigerian population's use of crypto assets grew, especially during the most extreme declines of the naira, in June and July 2023, according to Chainalysis[165]. The currency weakened to historic lows after President Bola Tinubu undertook some of the boldest reforms Nigeria had seen in years, including the removal of a popular but costly gasoline subsidy and the elimination of some exchange rate restrictions.

People are constantly looking for opportunities to hedge against the devaluation of their local currencies

---

[163] Young, M. (August 2, 2021). Aumenta la adopción de criptomonedas en Nigeria a pesar de las medidas de represión del gobierno. Cointelegraph. Accessed April 5, 2024, from https://es.cointelegraph.com/news/nigerian-crypto-adoption-rises-despite-govt-crackdown

[164] Reuters. (September 19, 2023). Nigeria's crypto usage is growing further, a report says. Accessed October 24, 2023, from https://www.reuters.com/technology/nigeria-crypto-usage-growing-further-report-says-2023-09-19/

[165] Idem.

and the persistent economic decline since COVID-19, which has been further exacerbated by the Fed's tightening policies, noted Moyo Sodipo, cofounder of Nigeria-based cryptocurrency exchange Busha[166].

Such is the boom in the use of crypto assets in Nigeria that in 2022, the country's financial regulator published a set of regulations for digital assets. Africa's most populous country was trying to find a middle ground between a total ban on crypto assets and their unregulated use[167].

In the Philippines, too, crypto assets have had a lot of impact, for a different reason. Filipinos started to earn extra money with a web3 game that uses a blockchain called Axie Infinity. In this game, users breed, fight, and trade pets called Axies. These are digital assets associated with a token whose value was increasing.

The game coincided with the pandemic, when many businesses in the Philippines collapsed. Some people were lucky enough to get Axies, which they were then able to sell and convert into fiat money. Some players reported earning as much as $300 to $400 a week. "Many people don't believe that you can

---

[166] Fathi, A. (June 20, 2024). Análisis: Cómo la política de tasas de la Reserva Federal impulsó la adopción de criptomonedas en África. FinanceFeeds. Accessed October 5, 2024, from https://financefeeds.com/es/analisis-de-como-la-politica-de-tasas-de-los-federales-impulso-la-adopcion-de-criptomonedas-en-africa/

[167] Reuters. (September 19, 2023). Nigeria's crypto usage is growing further, a report says. Accessed October 24, 2023, from https://www.reuters.com/technology/nigeria-crypto-usage-growing-further-report-says-2023-09-19/

make money playing a game, maybe for them it's too good to be true," explains one of the first Axie Infinity discoverers from the village, Art Art, in the documentary made by Play To Earn[168].

In South America as well, the use of cryptocurrencies is on the rise as a refuge against inflation. This is confirmed by 37% of the Argentine population, 42% in Peru, 41% in Colombia, and 37% in Chile, according to a study issued by Sherlock Communications [169] . That report also highlights Argentina as one of the first countries to accept salaries in crypto assets[170].

In view of Bill Gates's stance on Bitcoin and cryptocurrencies, one would think he would not allow his companies to use crypto assets. The truth is that Mr. Gates has tried to eradicate the crypto asset virus outside his house, but not inside. Microsoft, the company he founded, accepts Bitcoin as a means of

---

[168] El Economista. (May 16, 2021). Las criptomonedas sacan de la pobreza a un pueblo de Filipinas gracias a los videojuegos. Accessed April 6, 2024, from https://www.eleconomista.es/economia/noticias/11218302/05/21/Las-criptomonedas-sacan-de-la-pobreza-a-un-pueblo-de-Filipinas-gracias-a-los-videojuegos.html

[169] Ámbito. (August 23, 2023). El 37% de los argentinos cree que las criptomonedas ayudarán a combatir la inflación. Accessed November 1, 2023, from https://www.ambito.com/finanzas/el-37-los-argentinos-cree-que-las-criptomonedas-ayudaran-combatir-la-inflacion-n5801518

[170] Sherlock Communications. (n.d.). Blockchain Informe Latam 2023, Actualizaciones clave del ecosistema y la normativa en América Latina (p. 8).

payment for the purchase of applications and games[171].

They are also developing a wallet for use in their Edge browser in order to trade crypto assets [172]. Microsoft will also release more than 300 blockchain applications for use with Azure technology[173]. Although Bill Gates is not a director of the company he founded, it is striking that he allows Microsoft to employ as a means of payment a currency that generates deaths, is used to traffic drugs, is only for the rich, and is not profitable in the long term, as Mr. Gates himself has stated.

But it is not just Microsoft. Bill Gates, through his Gates Foundation, has launched a mobile payment solution using Bitcoin technology[174]. Bill Gates and the elites, on the one hand, bash the technology as

---

[171] Web Financial Group SA. (December 1, 2024). Microsoft ya acepta bitcoin para la compra de aplicaciones y juegos. Blog de finanzas y economía (Bankinter). Accessed October 24, 2023, from https://www.bankinter.com/blog/amp/lo-ultimo/microsoft-ya-acepta-bitcoin-para-la-compra-de-aplicaciones-y-juegos

[172] González, J. (March 18, 2023). Microsoft desarrolla una wallet de criptomonedas integrada a Edge. Criptonoticias. Accessed October 24, 2023, from https://www.criptonoticias.com/tecnologia/microsoft-desarrolla-wallet-criptomonedas-integrada-edge/

[173] Maldonado, J. (August 4, 2023). Microsoft tiene 300 soluciones blockchain en Azure, el doble que Amazon. Observatorio Blockchain. Accessed October 24, 2023, from https://observatorioblockchain.com/blockchain/microsoft-tiene-300-soluciones-blockchain-en-azure/

[174] Althauser, J. (October 20, 2017). La Fundación Gates lanza una solución de pagos móviles basada en blockchain. Cointelegraph. Accessed October 24, 2023, from https://es.cointelegraph.com/news/gates-foundation-launches-blockchain-based-mobile-payments-solution/amp

criminal and elitist, and on the other hand, they use it for their personal interests.

Another Bitcoin critic is Warren Buffett. He went so far as to claim that Bitcoin is "rat poison" and has "no intrinsic value"[175]. An in-depth study of this digital asset leads to the opposite conclusion. If it should be considered poison, it will rather be poison for the current financial system.

As I have already pointed out, Bitcoin has intrinsic value. Specifically, it is the world's most computer-supported payment system, which makes it more secure, efficient, decentralized, pseudonymous, and international, to name just some of its advantages. To reach this conclusion, once again, one must study the Bitcoin proposition.

Anyone would think that Warren Buffett, according to his own views, will not invest in anything related to crypto assets. It is curious because Warren Buffett himself acquired, for $1 billion in December 2021, a new bank called Nubank[176]. The surprise is that the bank allows users to exchange bitcoins and other

[175] Gallego, C. (April 14, 2023). Warren Buffett: "Bitcoin es como ir al casino, a la gente le encanta la idea de hacerse rica rápidamente". El Economista. Accessed April 6, 2024, from https://www.eleconomista.es/actualidad/noticias/12227234/04/23/warren-buffett-bitcoin-es-como-ir-al-casino-a-la-gente-le-encanta-la-idea-de-hacerse-rica-rapidamente.html

[176] Gola, Y. (February 15, 2022). Warren Buffett invierte mil millones de dólares en un neobanco amigable con Bitcoin, se deshace de acciones de Visa y Mastercard. Cointelegraph. Accessed October 6, 2024, from https://es.cointelegraph.com/news/warren-buffett-invests-1b-in-bitcoin-friendly-neobank-dumps-visa-and-mastercard-stocks

cryptocurrencies. Not only that, in early 2023, it launched its own cryptocurrency called nucoin[177]. The bank also has Easynvest, a trading platform that Nubank acquired in September 2020, and has been actively offering an exchange-traded fund, none other than a Bitcoin ETF, since June 2021. In 2023, Mr. Buffett earned some $130 million from his crypto banking investment[178].

Likewise, the official stream of thought does not report how banks position themselves with strong crypto investments. I already mentioned in Chapter 1 how many entities are collaborating with Ripple in the section on the Ripple Digital Law.

Among the entities with more investments[179], we can mention:

- Standard Chartered with $380 million and 6 investments in various projects. These include the Ripple blockchain network and Cobalt[180].

---

[177] Forbes Argentina. (October 13, 2023). Por qué Warren Buffett está operando silenciosamente con Bitcoin y otras crypto. Yahoo Finance. Accessed April 6, 2024, from https://es-us.finanzas.yahoo.com/noticias/warren-buffett-operando-silenciosamente-bitcoin-141900163.html

[178] Gola, Y. (October 31, 2023). Warren Buffett genera grandes beneficios con su holding en un banco favorable a las criptomonedas. Cointelegraph. Accessed October 31, 2023, from https://es.cointelegraph.com/news/warren-buffett-crypto-nu-stock-apple-amazon-2023-bitcoin

[179] Mozee, C. (August 15, 2021). These 13 banks have invested the most in crypto and blockchain to date. Business Insider. Accessed August 16, 2024, from https://markets.businessinsider.com/news/currencies/13-top-banks-investing-cryptocurrency-blockchain-technology-funding-blockdata-bitcoin-2021-8

[180] Cobalt is a UK based trading technology provider.

- BNY Mellon, with $321 million and 5 investments, including Fireblocks, a platform that allows financial institutions to issue, move, and store cryptocurrencies.

- Citibank, with $279 million and 14 investments, for example, in SETL, whose logging technology is used to move cash and other assets.

- UBS, with $266 million and 5 investments. The Swiss banking giant's portfolio includes Axoni, whose technology is used to modernize infrastructure in the capital markets.

- BNP Paribas, with $236 million and 9 investments, including Digital Asset to develop real-time trading and settlement applications using smart contracts based on the DAML programming language.

- Morgan Stanley, with $234 million and 3 investments, for example, in NYDIG, a cryptocurrency custody firm.

- JP Morgan Chase, with $206 million and 8 investments, including ConsenSys, an Ethereum software company.

- Goldman Sachs, with $204 million and 8 investments, including Coin Metrics, a blockchain data provider for institutional clients.

- MUFG, with $185 million and 6 investments. Japan's Mitsubishi UFJ Financial Group has invested in Coinbase, a U.S. cryptocurrency exchange, and Bitflyer, a Tokyo-based cryptocurrency exchange.

- ING, with $170 million and 6 investments, for example, HQLAx, a blockchain-based liquidity management platform.

- BBVA, with $167 million and 5 investments, for example, Covault, whose technology is used to store, share, and verify identities.

- Nomura, with $146 million and 5 investments, including Quantstamp, a blockchain security firm.

- Finally, Barclays, with $12 million and 22 investments, such as the company RealBlocks, a technology platform that connects advisors and investors with alternative investment managers.

Another bank that is friendly toward crypto assets is Singapore's DBS, for being an Ethereum whale. Specifically, its wallet address "0x9e...fb8e" is known, which holds 173,753 ETH worth approximately $651.5 million. According to Nansen, the wallet has generated an unrealized gain of more than $200 million from its ETH holdings[181].

---

[181] Pérez, H. (May 30, 2024). DBS, el banco más grande de Singapur, es una ballena de Ethereum: Nansen. Diario Bitcoin. Accessed August 16, 2024, from https://www.diariobitcoin.com/bancos-y-pagos-verticales/dbs-el-banco-mas-grande-de-singapur-posee-usd-650-millones-en-ethereum-nansen/

PayPal has launched its own stablecoin supported by U.S. dollars[182]. Finally, Coincub has published a list of the banks that favor crypto assets in its Crypto Banking Report 2024 [183]. Europe has 63 banks supporting the industry. North America is the second region with the most entities in the sector, with 30.

From all this data, we can conclude that banking is a money laundering machine, without very relevant consequences for it, unlike what happens to tools such as Tornado Cash. They try to sell us the story that both Bitcoin and crypto assets are dangerous, on the one hand, but on the other hand, they invest millions in crypto assets directly, as well as in companies in the sector. Finally, the central banks themselves are creating the cryptocurrency that they want us to use, the CBDCs, of course, regulated by them, not by the community.

This is the double standard at the center of the debate. The establishment is not necessarily opposed to technological change. It is opposed to change that it cannot supervise, tax, or reverse. When innovation threatens a monopoly, the first response is often moral panic, and the second response is capture.

---

[182] Roth, E., and Davis, W. (August 7, 2023). PayPal launches PYUSD stablecoin backed by the US dollar. The Verge. Accessed August 16, 2024, from https://www.theverge.com/2023/8/7/23822752/paypal-pyusd-stablecoin-cryptocurrency

[183] Otieno, N., and Bonniey, J. (2024). Crypto Banking Report 2024. Coincub. Accessed August 16, 2024, from https://coincub.com/ranking/crypto-banking-report-2024/

The elites and the powers that be are not necessarily opposed to technological change. They are opposed to it getting out of hand. Great revolutions, such as the present one, no matter how much some try to control them, produce great changes. Such was the case with the Industrial Revolution. It began in Great Britain at the end of the 18th century, transforming agricultural and artisanal societies into industrialized and urbanized ones. It was the beginning of the modern era, the end of which, for better or worse, we are witnessing today.

The Industrial Revolution took place in England because of an earlier political revolt, called the Glorious Revolution of 1688[184]. King James II was expelled from his country, and the new monarch, William of Orange, negotiated a new constitution with Parliament. From that moment on, monarchical power diminished. As a result, some decisions no longer depended exclusively on the king. This made it easier to adopt structural economic measures that provided incentives for investment, trade, and innovation. They reformed property rights, reduced and redistributed the tax burden, and passed laws that helped businesses[185].

They created the Bank of England in 1694, which helped finance the industry. It was a financial revolution that was the embers of what later became the fire of the Industrial Revolution. By the beginning of the 18th

---

[184] Acemoglu, D., and Robinson, J. A. (2012). Why Nations Fail (ch. 7, "The Turning Point"). Deusto: Kindle edition.

[185] Idem.

century, loans were available to anyone who could put up collateral. Two-thirds of these loans were granted, not to privileged social classes, but to merchants and businessmen. This meant economic inclusion in society. They also invested in infrastructure such as canals and roads that helped reduce transportation costs, another prerequisite for the Industrial Revolution to take place.

History reminds us that the internet revolution will overcome the resistance of elites and the powers that be. The manipulation and control we suffer today threaten two of the pillars of a society's growth: technology and education[186]. That is why official propaganda does not want people to make their own decisions. They want to keep them away from the new markets that new technologies offer. They are extractive institutions that do not allow technological change. They suppress economic incentives, which they try to control and stifle[187].

This is the lesson that the citizens of the 21st century must understand: neither the state nor the elites look after them. The official system watches over its own survival. New technologies are shaking the pillars of its power. This is why new forms of government and social organization will appear.

---

[186] Acemoglu, D., and Robinson, J. A. (2012). Why Nations Fail (cap.7 "The Turning Point"). Deusto: Kindle Edition. (Chapter 3. "The making of Prosperity and Poverty").

[187] Idem (Chapter 5. "I´ve seen the future, and it works: growth under extractive institutions")

A practical takeaway follows from this. If you want to understand whether an innovation is threatening entrenched power, look for coordinated messaging, regulatory bottlenecks, and the substitution of open systems with permissioned alternatives. Bitcoin's deeper challenge is not that it is volatile. It is that it changes who can verify, who can transact, and who must ask for permission.

CBDCs are often described as a digital version of cash, but their design can be fundamentally different from a permissionless network. A CBDC can be centralized, account-based, and programmable, which means access can be conditioned and transactions can be monitored under the rules of the issuer. Bitcoin, by contrast, is permissionless: no central administrator approves accounts, and its monetary policy is enforced by the network's consensus rules.

4. They do not want you to understand that Bitcoin reveals the defects of the financial system.

The oft-repeated and belligerent criticism of Bitcoin is meant to prevent us from understanding the virtues of the cryptoasset. Bitcoin exposes the weaknesses of the modern economy.

Bitcoin acts like a financial X-ray: it makes visible what the legacy system prefers to keep abstract, including the cost of settlement, the power of intermediaries, the hidden tax of inflation, and the fragility created by leverage and maturity mismatch.

To take one example, the technology that supports the legacy financial and banking system pales next to blockchain networks and cryptoassets.

Much of traditional finance still runs on siloed databases, batch processing, and layers of reconciliation across multiple ledgers. When money moves, it often moves as a message first, and settlement follows later. That gap creates friction, cost, and counterparty risk, especially across borders.

There was a time when banking innovated, like the aforementioned creation of the Bank of England in 1694, as a source of industrial funding[188].

---

[188] Acemoglu, D., and Robinson, J. A. (2012). Why Nations Fail (chap. 7 "The Turning Point"). Deusto: Kindle edition.

But banking payment technology now reflects a major technical and organizational lag. By maintaining a monopoly over critical rails, institutions have had little incentive to rebuild their infrastructure from the ground up.

An indisputable reference in this area is Dee Hock, a visionary in modern payment systems and the creator of VISA's first distributed structure. For him, "Bitcoin represents not only the future of payments, but also the future of governance"[189].

Dee Hock has openly criticized banking technology as outdated. Specifically, he believes that we are in the 21st century but still using 16th-century organizational structures. Bitcoin is one of the best examples of how a decentralized peer-to-peer organization can solve problems that these antiquated organizations cannot. Like the Internet, Bitcoin is not owned or controlled by a single entity, so it presents incredible opportunities for new levels of efficiency and transparency in financial transactions[190].

Hock's point is not that banks lack talent. It is that their architectures were designed for scarcity: limited hours, limited access, and centralized control. Bitcoin was designed for abundance: a network that runs

---

[189] Oro y Finanzas (May 26, 2015). Dee Hock, founder of Visa, joins the advisory board of the Bitcoin startup Xapo. Accessed October 24, 2023 from https://www.oroyfinanzas.com/2015/05/dee-hock-fundador-visa-consejo-asesor-startup-bitcoin-xapo/.

[190] Idem.

continuously, can be audited by anyone running a node, and can be joined without permission.

Bitcoin, in little more than a decade, has become one of the most resilient decentralized payment networks ever deployed. It reached hundreds of billions of dollars in market capitalization without a capital raise, with no marketing budget, no headquarters, and no paid executive team[191].

Its security does not come from a charter or a brand name. It comes from incentives and verification: miners compete to add blocks, nodes enforce the rules, and anyone can audit the monetary supply. In other words, trust shifts from institutions to open verification.

Another critic of the modern financial system is Jack Selby, vice president of corporate development in PayPal's early days. He noted in an interview that "one reason we were successful was that, no offense to the banks, we were competing with huge, bureaucratic, monolithic tanks that take forever to change"[192].

J. Christopher Giancarlo, former chairman of the U.S. Commodity Futures Trading Commission (CFTC), in his book *CryptoDad: The Fight for the Future of Money*, reflects on the current financial system and its

---

[191] Caballero, M., Ramió, A., and Carrera, M. (2020). Finanzas descentralizadas para inquietos. Cómo Blockchain y las DeFi cambiaron el sistema financiero para siempre (chap. 4). Editorial Bubok Publishing: Kindle edition.

[192] BBC (December 10, 2017). ¿Por qué los poderosos quieren un mundo sin dinero? Accessed October 31, 2023 from https://www.bbc.com/mundo/noticias-42272362.amp.

shortcomings. For example, he considers it archaic in check payments, settlement, shareholder, and proxy voting systems. It is also outdated in investor access, disclosure of information, and regulatory oversight of the financial system[193]. None of this is published by central banks in the reports in which they criticize Bitcoin.

These frictions help explain why many financial services feel digital on the surface but remain analog underneath. The user experience looks modern, but the back end still depends on intermediaries, reconciliation, and delayed settlement.

Furthermore, Barry Schuler, former CEO of the well-known dot-com company *America Online*, is critical of the modern financial system. He believes that the Internet has changed many retail businesses, from media to advertising. Yet financial services have largely remained untouchable. Banks simply built an interface layer for people to check accounts, while the infrastructure underneath stayed obsolete and archaic. Blockchain introduces a new token-based settlement system that can reshape traditional debt and equity markets[194].

---

[193] Giancarlo, C. J. (2021). CryptoDad: The Fight for the Future of Money ("Introduction"). Wiley.

[194] Roberts, J. J. (2020). Kings of Crypto: One Startup's Quest to Take the Cryptocurrency Out of Silicon Valley and onto Wall Street. Harvard Business Review Press.

Unlike Bitcoin and crypto assets, which are open to anyone who wants to use them, the banking and financial system is exclusionary and elitist. According to one study, roughly 30% of the world's population, about 2 billion people, does not have access to bank accounts. Of those who do have accounts, billions have very limited access, and many banks lack reliable access to international currencies, markets, or liquidity.

Bitcoin and crypto assets not only provide access to payment systems, but they also allow you to be your own bank. This principle is often captured in the motto "not your keys, not your coins," where control over private keys determines control over funds[195].

This shift also carries a hard truth: sovereignty demands competence. Losing keys, exposing seed phrases, or trusting the wrong custodian can be catastrophic. Yet the ability to self-custody, to use multisignature security, and to move value without permission creates an alternative that the legacy system cannot easily offer.

Bitcoin is for everyone, both for the elite of the first billion people and for the other billions[196]. Bitcoin and cryptocurrencies can provide financial and banking access to millions of people around the world. Far from being an asset only for the rich, it can be a financial lifeline for many poor people.

---

[195] Antonopoulos, A. (2017). El Internet del Dinero. Merkle Bloom LLC.

[196] Idem.

For Andreas Antonopoulos, in *The Internet of Money*, the reason for banking exclusion is that it cannot serve populations where there are no branches, in remote regions, for example. Both the adaptation to technology and the control exercised by the banking system over its clients are lacking. Regarding the latter, he stresses that the banking system needs to identify everyone at both ends of each transaction we carry out. For him, a totalitarian surveillance system has been built. This control system, which claims to guarantee our security, does not really pursue the eradication of poverty, but rather constant monitoring of our financial movements, including when we buy something as humble as a hamburger[197].

Part of the reason Bitcoin is unstoppable is that the world has a great need for this technology. Banks in the developed world cannot cost-effectively service many remote populations, and even where access exists, it often comes with high fees and tight control.

But perhaps the clearest deficiency that Bitcoin exposes in the current financial system is the inflation of legal tender, fiat currencies. One relevant fact that has gone largely unnoticed is how the U.S. Federal Reserve has modified consumer price index (CPI) methodologies over time. Saifedean Ammous refers to this in *The Fiat Standard: Debt Slavery as an Alternative to Human Civilization*.

---

[197] Idem.

The author refers to serious problems in measuring CPI. First, there is no definable unit of measurement, which leads to recurring disputes over what should be included in the base basket of goods. Second, there is no universally accepted way to interpret how prices adjust to technological improvements. Finally, the yardstick for measuring exchange rates is not stable, given that the unit used is the U.S. dollar, which is neither constant nor definable.

Ultimately, measuring CPI becomes a matter of subjective judgment, not numerical precision. Ammous quotes economist Stephen Roach, who began his career at the Federal Reserve in the 1970s. Roach acknowledged that then-chairman Arthur Burns fought inflation by eliminating from the CPI basket items whose prices were rising, while conveniently finding non-monetary explanations for those increases. By the time he was done, he had eliminated about 65% of the goods in the CPI, including food, oil, and energy-related products[198].

One of the most important ways in which CPI measurement has been manipulated has been through the elimination of housing prices from the market basket of goods, under the pretext that a house is an investment good, which is an absurd redefinition. Ammous concludes that the fiat standard first destroyed the ability of individuals to save, then forced

---

[198] Roach, S. S. (May 25, 2021). The Ghost of Arthur Burns. Project Syndicate. https://www.project-syndicate.org/commentary/fed-sanguine-inflation-view-recalls-arthur-burns-by-stephen-s-roach-2021-05

them to treat their own home as their savings account[199].

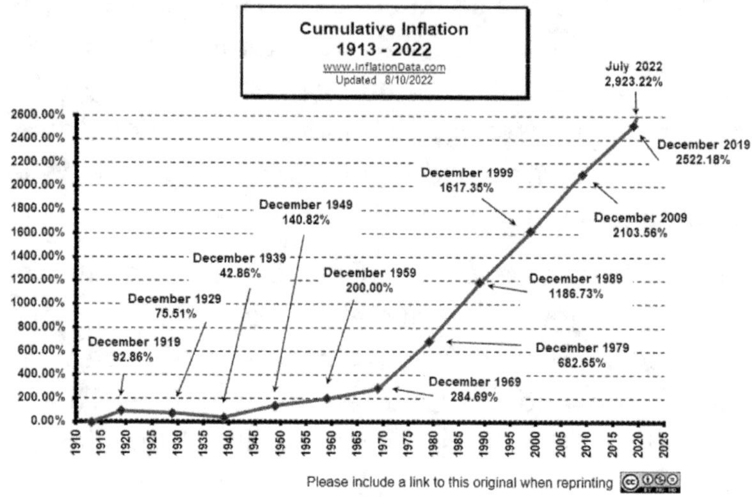

Fig. 12

The graph shows the relentless growth of inflation since the end of the gold standard in 1971, without taking into account the methodological changes referred to by Saifedean Ammous. Real inflation can be even higher.

But the official school of thought often blames these ills on the entrepreneur who ultimately raises prices[200].

---

[199] Ammous, S. (2021). The Fiat Standard: The Debt Slavery Alternative to Human Civilization. The Saif House: Kindle edition (chap. 4).

[200] Llamas, M. (September 1, 2023). Desmontando a la izquierda: la inflación no es culpa de las empresas. Libremercado. Accessed May 21, 2024 from

Indeed, the cryptoasset community is still immature. In this early stage, Internet sovereignty often depends on decentralization, yet decentralization does not eliminate human error, fraud, or short-term speculation. Even so, there will come a day when citizens understand that they have a decentralized tool to hedge against inflation. They will see, without intermediaries, that private money can operate with a predictable issuance policy. Then they will be able to choose economic freedom, meaning individual sovereignty.

Private money may return some of the wealth that states take away from citizens through monetary debasement. This argument was already put forward by the Nobel Prize-winning economist and a leading figure of Austrian economics, Friedrich von Hayek. In 1984, he stated:

"I don't believe we shall ever have good money again before we take the thing out of the hands of government. If we can't take it violently out of the hands of government, all we can do is, by some sly roundabout way, introduce something that they can't stop."[201]

---

https://www.libremercado.com/2023-09-01/desmontando-a-la-izquierda-la-inflacion-no-es-culpa-de-las-empresas-7045051/

[201] Hayek, F. A. (1984). Quoted in Institute of Economic Affairs (August 27, 2024). Freedom Week presentations: The Denationalisation of Money. https://iea.org.uk/freedom-week-presentations-the-denationalisation-of-money/

5. Difficulty in understanding the end of one era and the beginning of another

Our generation was born in the midst of a change of civilizations. We breathe out the smoldering end of the smokestacks of the Industrial Revolution, and breathe in the refreshing air of the beginning of the Internet Revolution.

We are fortunate not to have been born simply to be a stepping stone to industrial civilization. We can help create the civilization of the future. From our people will come the Rousseaus, Montesquieus, Lockes, or Newtons of the Internet Revolution.

It is difficult for us to comprehend the technological, social, and political changes in which we are immersed. Our mentality, designed in the patterns of the past, prevents us from seeing the future clearly.

Our time is at a turning point; it's like a threshold as we cross into a new room, leaving the old one behind without even noticing. We are in the blind spot of the change of civilizations. The variations that have taken place during our lifetime, although numerous, are not enough for us to perceive with all their transcendence the end of one epoch and the beginning of another.

Periods of transition are hard to diagnose from the inside. The basic facts are visible, but the meaning arrives late, once institutions, habits, and legal categories have already shifted. That delay is not a weakness of intelligence. It is a feature of human perception that treats slow change as background noise until it breaks into crisis.

This is not new; it has happened before in history, which repeats itself over and over again. Without going any further, the fall of the Roman Empire occurred officially for historians in the year 476 AD. From that year began an intermediate period, similar to the one we live in today. Centuries passed under the impression that everything went on as usual, under the languid power of the Roman Empire.

That is why Charlemagne was crowned Emperor of the Romans in the year 800[202] when it was already the Middle Ages. The same happened with the Renaissance (15th and 16th centuries). And the same happens today.

Some have pointed to the year 1914 as the year of the end of the West. Jacques Barzun, in his book "From Dawn to Decadence," considered that the great change took place when liberalism triumphed with the assumption that the best government is the one that governs the least. Since then, all Western nations have reformulated this ideal of liberty into liberality. The transformation has produced a semantic disorder. The substitution of liberalism for liberality was, in reality, just the opposite[203].

---

[202] On December 25, 800.

[203] Barzun, J. (2001). Del amanecer a la decadencia. Quinientos años de la vida cultural en Occidente (de 1500 a nuestros días). Taurus Historia.

This semantic drift is more than an academic dispute. When political language changes its meaning, legal concepts often follow, and citizens can be persuaded to accept measures they would have rejected under the older vocabulary.

Saifedean Ammous, in his book “The Bitcoin Standard,” analyzes the problem from another point of view. He considers that the classical liberal conception of government is associated with the abandonment by governments of sound money.

The reason is that sound money is a natural restraint against authoritarianism and government overreach. The year 1914, for Ammous, was the end of sound money. That is, the end of the economic responsibility of the state and its rulers, the consequences of which we suffer today.

The end of the gold standard at the beginning of World War I allowed governments to stop maintaining a balanced budget. State spending no longer had to be within the limits of tax revenues. Sound money imposed a dose of honesty and transparency on governments. It implied economic responsibility under the rule that consumption must come after production.

An unstable currency allows governments to act with impunity without having to present any bill to their people. The government can at any time increase the money supply to finance whatever it wants. Unlimited money printing generates inflation. In the years to come, when inflation has caused prices to rise, governments have blamed the destruction of the currency's value on multiple factors: the plotting of foreigners, bankers, local ethnic minorities, or past or future governments[204]. And as I have pointed out before, even companies[205].

When money can be created at will, law becomes the quiet partner of fiscal policy. Inflation not only raises prices. It also reallocates wealth, reshapes incentives, and pressures courts and legislators to justify interventions that would have been politically impossible under sound money.

The year to determine the end of the Industrial Revolution, and the beginning of the Internet Revolution is 1989[206]. Three very relevant events occurred: the fall of the Berlin Wall, the invention of the "WWW" by Tim Berners-Lee, and the peaceful demonstrations in China leading to the Tiananmen massacre.

Seen this way, nineteen eighty-nine is not just a political turning point. It is also a preview of the Internet's logic, where coordination can occur without centralized permission and where legitimacy is increasingly measured by results rather than hierarchy.

---

[204] Ammous, S. (2018). The Bitcoin standard. Deusto.

[205] Llamas, M. (September 1, 2023). Desmontando a la izquierda: la inflación no es culpa de las empresas. Libremercado. Accessed May 21, 2024 from https://www.libremercado.com/2023-09-01/desmontando-a-la-izquierda-la-inflacion-no-es-culpa-de-las-empresas-7045051/

[206] Among those who support this thesis: Davidson, J. D. and Rees-Mogg, W. ([2022] The Sovereign Individual: Mastering the Transition to the Information Age. Bubok. Kindle edition); Haass, R. ([2020] The World: a brief introduction. Penguin Press. New York. Kindle Edition).

The Industrial Revolution was a mass movement, managed by the ever-growing bureaucracy of the Modern State, the largest mass management apparatus in history. The three events referred to above that occurred in 1990 are precisely mass movements. The fall of the Berlin Wall and the Tiananmen Uprising are two examples of the weakness of the Modern State. The peaceful destruction of the wall is not only the defeat of the USSR or of Communism in the old continent.

It was the uprising of the masses against the tyranny of the state hierarchy. The governments of the future will increasingly resemble the model of the Internet rather than the Modern State. The third mass movement was the peer-to-peer, stateless relationship of the World Wide Web.

The Internet Revolution is taking place faster than all previous Revolutions. The first Revolution was the cognitive one carried out by Homo sapiens over hundreds of thousands of years. Homo sapiens populated East Africa about 150,000 years ago. They came to coexist with other human species, such as the Neanderthals. They spread out over the rest of the planet about 70,000 years ago[207]. And survived. The other hominid species disappeared.

Homo sapiens was not the strongest hominid species, but it was certainly the most intelligent. Their main ability was, and still is, their ability to reason and

---

[207] Harari, Y. N. (2011). "Sapiens". Debate. Chapter 2. Kindle Edition.

innovate. They came up with new objects that were more practical, used new technologies, discovered new methods, and developed more complex ideas that allowed them to abstract reality[208]. Because of this special ability, they wereable to adapt to new environments, overcome difficulties, and actively transform the world in which they lived. Their intelligence also allowed them to cooperate ef efficiently to organize themselves into even larger communities. Homo sapiens are thinkers and inventors. It was the ability to innovate that allowed humans to dominate the earth and fulfill what some people consider to be a part of a divine plan[209].

The second great Revolution was the Agricultural Revolution, which trans formed the previous hunters and gatherers. They wandered from place to place in search of food. There was no concept of ownership of land, because it was not tilled. Nor about housing, since they did not live stably in the same place.

A few tools and weapons were enough to live. Carrying more goods than necessary was a hindrance. There was little or nothing to steal[210].

---

208 Homo sapiens developed agricultural techniques and domesticated animals. They invented writing and money. They have deepened and developed areas such as science, mathematics, engineering, and medicine. They have created culture and philosophy.

209 Book of Genesis of the Bible.

210 Davidson, J. D. and Rees-Mogg, W. (2022). The sovereign individual: Mastering the Transition to the Information Age. Bubok Publishing (Madrid): Kindle edition.

As for the time spent working, it was enough to live on. The opposite was a problem since carrying too many goods could make it impossible to find food in the future. In some groups, those who hunted excessively were punished with exile. Members of a typical hunter-gatherer community might work as little as eight to fifteen hours a week[211].

Agriculture, like the Internet today, brought about a great revolution in the or ganization of economic, cultural, and legal life. Crops and domestic animals raised by farmers were valuable assets that had to be stored, accumulated, accounted for, and inventoried. In addition, they had to be protected, since they could be stolen.

Farmers were subject to looting at harvest time, which increased violence and defense of assets[212].

As is happening today with the Internet Revolution, the move to an agricultural society transformed the law. At that time, private property, the pillar of civil law, emerged. It was an inevitable consequence of settlement on agricultural land.

It also, like today, changed the economic organization, which began to revolve around the village[213].

---

211 Idem.

212 Idem. It also, like today, changed the economic organization, which began to revolve around the village96.

213 Davidson, J. D. and Rees-Mogg, W. (2022). The sovereign individual: Mastering the Transition to the Information Age. Bubok Publishing (Madrid): Kindle edition.

In the Agricultural Revolution, property was acquired by prolonged possession. In the modern registry system, developed in the 19th century, ownership was based on registration. Possession was relegated to the background. The Internet Revolution is giving possession back its lost prominence. There are no records of ownership in the blockchain, but possession of the keys that give access to the wallets of cryptoassets.

This is why the custody of keys becomes a legal and practical frontier. In traditional systems, a registry can cure mistakes, reverse fraud, or clarify title. In cryptoasset systems, the operational reality is harsher: control of the key is often control of the asset, and remedies may depend more on technical recovery than on paperwork.

The third revolution was the Industrial Revolution, which took place at the end of the 18th century. The book "The Third Wave," written by Alvin Toffler, summarizes very well the social and economic effects of this revolution, the end of which we are witnessing today.

For Toffler, the model on which the Industrial Revolution revolved was the factory. Men who had spent the last 10,000 years tilling the soil and living in their huts were destined for the factories. This process took place in a record period of less than 300 years.

However, then as now, the new generations had to be prepared for their new role. In particular, productive men were needed in the factories at that time. Andrew

Ure, a physician of that period, noted that it was "nearly impossible to turn people past the age of puberty, whether drawn from rural or from handicraft occupations, into useful factory workers"97. Therefore, a new type of education, "mass" based in factories and assembly lines, began.

The closest thing to a "school" of the Industrial Revolution is precisely a factory. Millions of students have been molded on a large scale on the assembly lines of the schools by teacher-like operators. The end product has been millions of people trained under the same template, regardless of their personal particularities.

Those of us born before the change, that is, before 1990, have inherited this type of teaching. In my case, I can cite such industrial practices from several of my own former teacher-minions of the education system: smacks on the head, pulling my sideburns, public ridicule, and even a bite on the ear for my consummate incompetence in learning arithmetic at the age of seven! Thankfully, the Internet Revolution is changing this conception of uniform teaching. However, we are still a long way from the desired "personalized teaching," as the patterns of the past are still in place, albeit to a lesser extent.

In our times, the personal characteristics of the learner are beginning to be taken into account. In the industrial era, hyperactivity and/or attention deficit disorders, anxiety, gifted children with needs, or highly sensitive persons (HSP) had not been diagnosed. The magic educational formula that solved all these adaptation problems was the cane, a loud slap, a kick, or worse. The present generations no longer have to follow the same replicable, repressive, and standardized model.

The education of the Internet Revolution is and will be more and more about the home and less and less about the factory.

The technology of the Internet Revolution demands training that differs drastically from that offered in the Industrial Revolution. Tools such as Artificial Intelligence will save labor and time, and will require redefining the qualities of the worker while offering new jobs. The classic model of uniformity for the factory is obsolete. The most qualified person will not be the one who conforms most closely to a pattern, but the one who is the most cultured, mature, andable to decide between a large number of tools at his or her disposal. Training based on giving mechanical answers typical of the industrial era will no longer make sense.

Another change that will occur and that we are already witnessing is that there will be more job flexibility. The factory is based on a face-to-face working relationship. In the Internet Revolution, work is based on a results-based relationship, no matter where. Many jobs can already be performed from the worker's home, and schedules are and will be increasingly flexible.

The Industrial Revolution necessitated standardization, which is gradually ceasing today. Standard education, standard production, and standard ways of measuring[214]. Millions of identical products were destined for mass consumers.

Many still drink the same thing (Coca-Cola), eat the same thing (McDonald's), and buy the same thing all over the world. All measurements were also standardized in a new metric system, and a new calendar was created in the French Revolution. The Internet Revolution is changing the principle of standardization[215].

Companies born in the Industrial Revolution must adapt to the new civilization. An example of positive change is the textile company Zara. Far from mass producing millions of identical T-shirts, it prepares its products according to the millions of daily data points it collects from its stores. Its products are now produced according to the patterns of the Internet Revolution. Zara only makes what its consumers want, so its stores adapt to those needs. In short, no two stores are identical. This is the change we are witnessing: from mass production to the production of customized products.

Factory work also demanded specialization, leaving the moonlighter in danger of extinction. The most efficient and manageable thing to do was for one

---

[214] The French Revolution created and unified the ways of measuring.

[215] Toffler, Alvin (1980). The third wave. Plaza & Janes Publishers.

person to specialize in a particular area. Experts began to proliferate like mushrooms after a heavy rain.

Society was further fragmented into millions of interconnected parts: factories, churches, schools, unions, prisons, hospitals, and the like. To fit the various separate pieces of society together, integration specialists, i.e., managers and executives, emerged. Thus, bureaucracy, red tape, and organizational structures were other characteristics of the Industrial Revolution[216].

For Visa's founder, Dee Hook, the increase in state power, industrialization, and Cartesian theories led to the emergence of hierarchical organizations and institutions. They are centralized institutions where compliance with inefficient protocols is rewarded, sacrificing individual initiative and ultimately creativity[217].

For the Industrial Revolution, the French Revolution, and the Modern State, the individual is ultimately, like an atom, part of a whole. For them, the institution is above the individual, be it the state, the company, the organization, or even the religious institution.

The industrial manager learned that mass production was the most advanced and efficient way to produce. The mass market required standardized

---

[216] Idem.

[217] Hock, D. (2005). One from Many VISA and the Rise of Chaordic Organization. Berrett-Koehler.

goods and masses of equal workers that could be moved with uniform incentives. The effective manager learned that synchronization, centralization, maximization, and concentration were necessary in order to achieve their goals[218].

With the Industrial Revolution, life revolved around machines that workers had to attend to on time. The era of "synchronization" began, which Charles Chaplin masterfully reflected in the movie "Modern Times". Working life extrapolated this principle to school, hospitals, family life, etc. The concept of "time" before this Revolution was relative, i.e., reducible or extensible. From the emergence of factories, civilization began to live the same schedules for the first time in history[219]. At present, and especially after COVID-19, these trends are also changing. Teleworking was unthinkable just a few years ago. The Industrial mentality made it inconceivable for us to work from home or to keep different hours than the rest of our colleagues.

Factories also generated two other characteristics, concentration (everyone in the same place) and centralization around institutions, companies, and ultimately the nation-state. Political power and economic power came together. That is why Central Banks controlled by the rulers themselves were

---

[218] Toffler, Alvin (1980). The third wave. Plaza & Janes Publishers

[219] Idem.

created. The Nation State is the union of the political system and the economic system[220].

The Modern State, with the Industrial Revolution and the French Revolution [221] produced the management of the masses. All people began to receive the same messages and the same images: Lenin with his prominent jaw under a red background, Chaplin with a bowler hat and a cane, Churchill making the victory sign, or Marilyn Monroe with her flounced skirt[222].

The Internet Revolution, on the contrary, is decentralizing information and messages. States are trying at all costs to control the media born in the Internet Revolution. The United States issued a law to try to put an end to TikTok use within its jurisdiction. In addition, the control by States of social networks worldwide affected at least 250 million people in 2021. Elon Musk recently denounced on the social network "X" the European Commission's attempt to censor content from its users. He specifically noted, "The European Commission offered an illegal secret deal: if we discreetly censored speech without telling anyone, we wouldn't be fined. The other platforms accepted the deal. He didn't."

---

[220] The word "international" was coined by Jeremy Bentham in 1789, the same year as the French Revolution. In the Internet age, the concept of the nation is becoming less central; relations are increasingly "extra-national".

[221] Idem.

[222] Ortega and Gasset, José (1930). The revolt of the masses.Tecnos. Own translation.

Pavel Durov, founder and CEO of Telegram, was arrested on August 24, 2024, and faces up to 20 years in prison for allegedly enabling various crimes on his platform. Pavel Durov has always defended the privacy of his Telegram. Many people have cried out in the face of the attacks on privacy that the West is undergoing. Decentralized social networking proposals may be the best defense against state attacks on privacy, as proposed by "Warpcast"[223]. The Modern State has finally taken off its mask. The Modern State is the modern inquisition.

Ortega y Gasset reflected on "the masses" in his work "The Revolt of the Masses". The work refers to the false principle of equality that justifies the masses. This equality "sweeps away everything that is different, ungrateful, individual, qualified, and select. Whoever is not like everyone else runs the risk of being eliminated. And it is clear that this "everyone" is not "everyone"[224]. As I have already pointed out, the Internet Revolution rests on a technical, not ideological, equality that allows peer-to-peer relationships to create law and transfer value and information.

For Ortega y Gasset, the mass is made up of the vulgar man[225], who feels he has acquired rights without

---

[223] https://warpcast.com/

[224] https://warpcast.com/

[225] Ortega and Gasset, José (1930). The revolt of the masses. Tecnos. Own translation.

effort[226]. The State desperately needs an equal and malleable mass. Likewise, the mass needs to rest their vital responsibility on the State[227]. Therefore, society lives for the State, for the machine of government[228].

The mass-man regards the State as his own. Specifically, "he sees it, he admires it, he knows that it is there, ensuring his life; but he is not aware that it is a human creation invented by certain men and sustained by certain virtues and assumptions that were there yesterday in men and that may evaporate tomorrow."

The mass-man sees in the State an anonymous power, and as he "feels himself anonymous (vulgo), he believes that the State is his own thing. Imagine that any difficulty, conflict, or problem arises in the public life of a country: the human masses will tend to demand that the State should immediately take charge of it, that it should take direct charge of resolving it with its gigantic and incontrovertible means.

---

[226] Ortega and Gasset also add that the mass man considers himself entitled to give his opinion on any matter, without prior effort. The mass man feels perfect, but not for himself, but out of vanity. He seeks in others the idea he has of himself. A fictitious, imaginary, and problematic idea.

[227] Ortega and Gasset consider mass man as "lives without weight and without roots that allow themselves to be dragged along by the slightest current. It is the age of currents, and of letting oneself be dragged along". Own translation.

[228] Ortega and Gasset, José (1930). The revolt of the masses.Tecnos. In the portentous machine work. The mass says: "The State is me", which is a perfect mistake.

The greatest danger threatening our civilization is:

The statification of life, the interventionism of the State, the absorption of all social spontaneity by the State; that is to say, the annulment of historical spontaneity, which ultimately sustains, nourishes, and drives human destinies. When the mass feels some misfortune or, simply, some strong appetite, it is a great temptation for it that a permanent and sure possibility of obtaining everything without effort, struggle, doubt, or risk- without more than touching the spring and making. Historically, it has been the technical changes that have modified in a very relevant way the established power. The book "The Sovereign Individual, written by James Dale Davidson and William Rees-Mogg, refers to some examples.

Chivalry was the main cause of the feudal revolution. It arose not for ideological reasons, as we often think. The beginning of this revolution was technical: the discovery of the stirrup, the nailed iron horseshoe, the contoured saddle, the spur, and the bridle. It became impossible for the peasant landowner to finance a horse and armor. They had to rally around a Count or lord who would protect them in exchange for caring for and cultivating their land.

As "The Sovereign Individual" points out, there are two technical discoveries that led to the creation of the Modern States: the cannon and the printing press. The appearance of the first firearms in Europe took place in the 14th century. The use of gunpowder in the Western military gradually transformed the techniques of warfare.

These technological and tactical changes significantly affected the European battlefields. The horse, so relevant in feudalism, lost its importance. Instead, another instrument appeared, the cannon, which changed the course of history. It was the main reason for the fall of Constantinople on May 29, 1453. This event marked the end of the Byzantine Empire and is commonly seen as the close of the Middle Ages and the beginning of the Renaissance and the Modern Age in Europe[229].

Likewise, the discovery of the printing press by Johannes Gutenberg in the 15th century marked the beginning of the mass information age.

The Internet Revolution is disrupting this static model of organization based on the modern state. The effective, barrier-free, peer-to-peer transmission of information and value requires new forms of governance.

In the Industrial Revolution, decisions did not require the speed that the Internet Revolution requires today. In the industrial age, a message could take a week to travel from Boston to Philadelphia. Today it takes only seconds. Our leaders, forced to work

---

229 The conquest was carried out with cannons that were previously carried with great effort and technique by land. The walls of Constantinople, although robust, could not resist the prolonged bombardment of the Ottoman artillery. It is also interesting to note the relationship of the fall of Constantinople with the rise of Moscow as the "Third Rome".

through the institutions of a slower society, cannot produce intelligent decisions as quickly as events require. Decisions usually come too late.

Today's political structures are obsolete. This is true regardless of the ideology of the political party in office. They are inadequate institutions in terms of scale, structure, and speed.

Our political systems are copied from models invented before the advent of canned food, refrigeration, gas lights, photography, the oven, the typewriter, the telephone, and, of course, before the computer and the Internet. Perhaps this is the most important major political problem we are facing: the obsolescence of our most basic political and governmental institutions[230].

One of the clearest examples was COVID-19. The Lancet Commission issued a report in 2022, in which it highlighted the global response failures related to the pandemic [231] . Among others, it cites widespread failures in prevention, transparency, rationality, public health practices, operational cooperation, and international solidarity. The report estimates that 17.7 million deaths worldwide could have been avoided. It further notes that most national governments were unprepared and too slow in their response. They paid too little attention to the most vulnerable groups, and

---

[230] Toffler, Alvin (1980). The third wave. Plaza & Janes Publishers.

[231] The report can be downloaded here:
https://www.thelancet.com/pdfs/journals/lancet/ PIIS0140-6736(22)01585-9.pdf

did not cooperate with each other. The report not only criticizes governments, but also takes aim at the WHO for its slowness in declaring the pandemic and recognizing airborne transmission of the virus.

This unfortunate example shows us that the political challenges of the Internet Revolution force us to face the problems of more decentralized, participatory, and diverse societies.

In a networked society, governance is judged on speed, clarity, and credibility. Delayed decisions do not remain neutral. They compound harm, invite misinformation, and fracture compliance, especially when citizens can compare outcomes across jurisdictions in real time.

Modern states, like a drowning man on the verge of death fighting for his survival, will cling tightly to the raft of surveillance and manipulation. They will try their best to establish a system of absolute control, but will ultimately fail. When the community matures and becomes aware of the sovereign tools available to them, thanks to the Internet, States will have no choice but to adapt and change to stop being inefficient and bureaucratic. The institutional overload based on inflation and tax increases will not be sustainable in the medium term. The political system will not be able to suck more resources from its citizens. Modern political work requires convincing the citizen that such extraction is necessary for the common good. This model has an expiration date.

Likewise, being born in a certain place or being a national of a certain country will be anecdotal. Choosing the right jurisdiction (State) to apply the Digital Laws issued on the Internet will be the most relevant. New techniques are changing the way we do business. Never before have so many been so connected from various parts of the world. State localism cannot meet the challenges of the new transactional economies.

The individual will cease to be national and will be sovereign. He will be able to choose which state to submit to, overcoming localism and state coercion. New moral rules will emerge in accordance with the new times, those of the Internet. Those companies, persons, or organizations that do not adapt to the new dictates will be left behind. The State that wants to survive will have no choice but to slim down and return to its essence: to properly protect the lives of its citizens, property rights, and administer effective justice.

In practical terms, "being sovereign" in a digital economy means controlling the tools that let you transact, communicate, and store value across borders. That includes operational control, such as key management and secure authentication, and legal control, such as choosing predictable jurisdictions, clear dispute-resolution mechanisms, and transparent rules for taxation and enforcement. As exit becomes easier, states will compete more on competence, trust, and service quality than on coercion.

III. The Birth of Digital Law

"If clams can be money, furs can be money, gold can be money, and so on, if money is not just coins or notes issued by a government under legal tender laws, but rather can be a wide variety of objects, then just what is money anyway?"

Nick Szabo, "The Origins of Money" (2002).

1. Digital Law and Commercial Law

The great revolutions discussed in Chapter 2 have drastically changed our lives, the way we organize ourselves in society, and the law itself.

Each era, according to its socioeconomic circumstances, has its own legal system. Property law arose as a result of the settlement of agricultural societies. Commercial law was born in the Middle Ages with the increase in trade between different kingdoms. Corporate law germinated in the 17th century thanks to maritime mercantile trade[232]. Labor law appeared among the assembly lines of the factories of the Industrial Revolution. Digital law and tokenization[233] are two of the pillars of the law of the Internet Revolution.

In this chapter, "digital law" refers to rule systems that are enforced primarily by software and distributed consensus rather than by a territorial sovereign. When rules are embedded in an open protocol, compliance is verified by the network itself, which makes the rule set global in scope, predictable in operation, and difficult to modify unilaterally.

The law of the Internet Revolution resembles the birth of commercial law in the Middle Ages. First, both bodies of law emerged around the issuance of a hard

[232] Mainly in Holland and England.

[233] Or the securitization of assets into tokens.

currency. Commercial law gained momentum after the creation of the florin in 1252. It was the first stable currency in Europe since the aureus of Julius Caesar[234]. Digital law and Internet law are emerging after the issuance of the first Internet currency, Bitcoin, which is projected to increase in value over the long term.

In the Middle Ages, Florence was the commercial center of Europe, and the florin became the main instrument of exchange on the continent. Thanks to it, its citizens accumulated wealth by trading with a solid currency. Holders of the florin acquired the freedom to work, produce, trade, and prosper. Venice followed Florence's example, issuing its own hard currency, the ducat, in 1270.

By the end of the 14th century, more than 150 European cities and states had minted such coins. This financial stability generated the political, scientific, intellectual, and cultural prosperity of the Italian city-states, and it later spread throughout Europe. It is no coincidence that Florentine and Venetian authors were leaders of the cultural Renaissance. The conclusion is clear: history shows that a sound monetary standard is a precondition for human prosperity[235]. This new wealth clustered around cities, which were centers of

---

[234] Vargas Vasserot, C. (2012). La evolución histórica del derecho mercantil y su concepto. Universidad de Almería.

[235] Ammous, S. (2018). The Bitcoin Standard. Deusto.

political, religious, and commercial activity from which mercantile law would emerge.

The parallel is not merely historical. A durable monetary standard lowers transaction frictions, reduces the premium that market participants charge for uncertainty, and makes longer-term agreements practical. In that environment, merchants can innovate in contracts, credit instruments, and dispute resolution, and those innovations then pressure the legal system to adapt.

Second, the merchants of the Middle Ages had to organize themselves in a new way through professional associations linked to municipalities. Members took an oath to abide by the statutes, obey the consuls, and conduct themselves in an orderly manner. These corporations protected their associates and economic interests, dictated regulations, and ultimately created a new jurisdiction with regulatory autonomy and dispute resolution. Magistrates watched over corporate interests, interpreted the laws, and exercised jurisdictional functions[236].

At the dawn of digital Internet law, communities related to new technologies, mainly blockchain and artificial intelligence, must create new forms of governance that align with the decentralized rules of Internet jurisdiction. These are new horizontal

---

236 Vargas Vasserot, C. (2012). La evolución histórica del derecho mercantil y su concepto. Universidad de Almería.

institutions, distinct from the vertical and disjointed model of the modern state.

Institutions that arise from the community itself, and that help organize the free issuance of digital laws and private regulations; institutions that favor digital commerce, protect the interests of members, and resolve disputes that may arise between them. That is precisely the proposal of the Blockchain Arbitration & Commerce Society (BACS)[237].

BACS offers, among other services, the creation of private standards for the community, the defense of members' interests, and the resolution of disputes arising from Internet-based technologies.

In practical terms, these community institutions can function as connective tissue between protocol rules and real-world consequences. They can publish standards, certify best practices, and provide arbitration frameworks that are legible to courts and regulators while still respecting the underlying peer-to-peer architecture of the Internet.

Third, both in the Middle Ages and today, the inadequacy of existing law to meet new commercial needs in light of technical and economic realities is obvious. In the Middle Ages, the law applicable to emerging commercial needs was the so-called ius commune, made up of Roman and canon law.

---

237 Blockchain Arbitration & Commerce Society (BACS). www.bacsociety.com

It was necessary to create a new, agile, and flexible body of law, later called lex mercatoria. It was based on equity, transactional security, credit, and the protection of good faith. It developed its own principles, new normative sources, its own jurisdictional order, and completely new legal institutions.

Commercial disputes were resolved with arbitrators, often lawyers or attorneys, called magistrates. The traditional Roman-canonical jurisdiction was not prepared to resolve the emerging commercial disputes [238] . Official powers began to recognize the validity of private magistrates' decisions, as the Catholic Monarchs did with the Consulate of Burgos on July 21, 1494[239].

The current legal systems of nation-states are not equipped to accommodate the proposals brought forth by new technologies. They will be as outdated for the commerce emerging from the Internet Revolution as canon law once was for the commerce of the Middle Ages.

An essential right that is already being superseded by Bitcoin and other digital laws is ownership based on registration in public records. Registration records the

---

[238] Vargas Vasserot, C. (2012). La evolución histórica del derecho mercantil y su concepto. Universidad de Almería.

[239] Idem. Specifically, they established: "We hereby grant license, power, and jurisdiction to the said Prior and Consuls of the Merchants of the said City of Burgos.. so that they may know and hear the differences, debates, and pending disputes.. so that they may decide them briefly and summarily, according to the style of the Merchants, without giving rise to delays, nor malice, nor time limits for lawyers.." (own translation).

owner of the property, the title of acquisition[240], and any encumbrances, such as mortgage loans. Registry law also resolves discrepancies that may arise between the registered owner and a person claiming to be the real owner. In this system, public notaries certify the veracity of the information.

A typical case is that of the third-party mortgagee. If a person acquires mortgaged real estate in good faith and without knowledge of an unregistered real right, the law may protect that person under certain circumstances. These registry rules do not apply to Bitcoin, which has its own effective rules within Internet jurisdiction.

In Bitcoin, there is no third-party mortgage; there is either access or no access to the keys of a wallet. The "not your keys, not your coins" rule means that without your keys, there are no coins. In practice, Bitcoin is its own registry. It works more efficiently, transparently, and cheaply than state registries. Moreover, it is a more secure registry system than any traditional registry because it is continuously audited by the network.

A striking example of the collision between Bitcoin and the legal order of our world is the case of James Howells, a computer engineer who mistakenly threw away a hard drive containing 7,500 bitcoins. Mr. Howells, of course, could not go to a land registry to reclaim his bitcoins. He applied for access to the municipal landfill site at Newport City Council

[240] For example, a sale or a donation.

(Wales)[241]. The official on duty denied access "under our environmental permit, and that work of that nature would have a huge negative environmental impact on the surrounding area"[242]. Being unable to recover 7,500 bitcoins, or about $275 million[243], from a landfill on environmental grounds is proof of the inadequacy of state regulation.

Another problem that state rules cannot solve in connection with Bitcoin and cryptoassets is forced confiscation. The Bitcoin blockchain records all Bitcoin transactions. Each unit of bitcoin is associated with a wallet (public address) that can be accessed only with a private key.

No matter how many times a judge orders the seizure of a cryptoasset deposited in a decentralized wallet, or how many law enforcement officers are sent to a person's home, the coins cannot be seized. Only cryptoassets deposited in centralized entities (exchanges) can be seized. The only effective method today for recovering digital assets stored in

---

[241] Cáceres, I. (December 17, 2021). El hombre que tiró a la basura un disco duro con 387 mil millones de euros en bitcoins pide ayuda a la NASA. Business Insider. Accessed October 31, 2023 from https://www.businessinsider.es/hombre-tiro-387-millones-bitcoins-basura-pide-ayuda-nasa-982399

[242] Protos Staff. (September 8, 2023). The owner of 8K Bitcoin lost in the landfill threatens to bankrupt the local council. Protos. Accessed October 31, 2023, from https://protos.com/owner-of-8k-bitcoin-lost-in-landfill-threatens-to-bankrupt-local-council/

[243] At the time of writing, the value of one Bitcoin was $36,654.90.

decentralized wallets is not judicial execution, but physical coercion.

Unfortunately, torture has been used in the past and in the present, and it appears likely to persist wherever legal systems remain technically incapable of enforcement.

This asymmetry between legal title and technical control is one of the defining tensions of the Internet Revolution. When possession is expressed as control of cryptographic keys, enforcement depends less on paper orders and more on custody practices, key management, and the security model chosen by the user.

As was the case in the Middle Ages, a new trade, digital, is being born, even if we are not always aware of it. For example, in February 2024, I had the opportunity to attend the Web Summit in Doha, Qatar. One roundtable addressed "marketing in the time of tokenization." One of the expert speakers was Robby Young (CEO of Animoca Brands)[244]. He summarized the essence of tokenization in video games by highlighting the possibility for players to become owners of the weapons and other digital assets they use when playing. Thus, there is a difference in focus between a traditional video game and a Web 3.0 game. A traditional video game aims to entertain its players.

[244] Other speakers included Bozena Rezab (CEO of Gamee), Simone Berry (CEO of POCLab), and the panel was moderated by Sonya Barlow (writer and BBC contributor).

A Web 3.0 video game is based on play to earn, that is, to play to win, not only to enjoy.

For traditional players, play-to-earn is meaningless. What matters is that the game is good and entertaining. But the emerging cryptoasset community finds in play to earn a space for entertainment and speculation. This creates previously unimaginable options: exchanging digital assets between players, selling assets for a profit, or ending a game by monetizing digital assets obtained after many hours of effort.

After the roundtable, I met Robby Young at a private event. I remarked that, at heart, his talk was closer to a digital law class than a marketing class. We agreed that tokenization is a new way to securitize property rights, for example, through the representation of a weapon or a skill in a token or an NFT. We also discussed the change occurring in property law itself. In traditional law, ownership is based on registration in a registry. In digital law, what matters is possession. In a sense, we are returning to the origins of property law.

It is striking that a person like Robby, who has a degree in art, is aware of the legal change taking place. For many traditional lawyers, tokens and wallets can feel as unreal as watching an animated film. The truth is that there is nothing more tangible than a digital asset on a public blockchain, because it creates enforceable constraints that do not depend on anyone's permission.

Any lawyer who started practicing before the fall of the Berlin Wall has probably faced only three major technological shifts: replacing the typewriter with the computer, commissioning a website to advertise an office, and downloading WhatsApp.

As happened in the Middle Ages with commercial law, we are witnessing an Internet-native law. It is now possible to buy cryptoassets from a decentralized wallet, use tokenized assets in a video game, or exchange assets on a decentralized exchange. These are ways to exercise ownership under the new rules of the Internet Revolution. In short, the Internet Revolution, as in other times, is creating its own law.

2. From Law in Stone to Law in Blockchain

From a historical point of view, the drafting of laws has required various materials such as stone, paper, clay, or papyrus. With the advent of computers, rules began to be deployed in computer programs under the idea that "code is law." Today, we are witnessing the issuance of digital laws that operate within Internet jurisdiction.

A key difference is that the Internet can distribute and verify rules at nearly zero marginal cost, while blockchains can also coordinate agreement about shared state, such as balances, ownership claims, and permissions. When combined with smart contracts, a blockchain can behave like a rulebook that executes itself whenever predefined conditions are met.

The oldest extensive legal text that has come down to us is the Code of Hammurabi from 1760 BCE[245]. It regulated a set of 282 laws inscribed on a stone issued by the Babylonian King Hammurabi (1795 to 1750 BCE), who conquered and later reigned over ancient Mesopotamia.

This code regulated the Law of Talion, known by its rule of "an eye for an eye, a tooth for a tooth"[246]. The aim was to establish proportionality between the harm

---

[245] Vargas Vasserot, C. (2012). La evolución histórica del derecho mercantil y su concepto. Universidad de Almería.

[246] It is enshrined in Exodus 21:23-25, Leviticus 24:18-20, and Deuteronomy (Old Testament).

suffered by the victim and the punishment to be applied. The rule was intended to reduce the desire for revenge suffered by victims or their loved ones. Repaying violence with violence is an evil that, both in the past and today, can destroy a society[247].

Disregarding the normative content and taking a purely technical point of view, the most interesting feature of this Code is that its rules were engraved in stone and could not be erased, changed, or manipulated. Everyone could access the regulation, creating an environment of predictability: no one could claim not to know the rule and then take justice into their own hands. Despite the major differences between stone and blockchain, both seek the security that comes from preventing unilateral modification or manipulation.

Another famous set of rules carved in stone was the Ten Commandments that Yahweh gave to Moses. According to the book of Exodus in the Bible, the legislator of this rule was God himself. Stone was used to ensure permanence and durability. The Bible also holds that the Ten Commandments are imprinted in the conscience of all men by virtue of God's covenant with mankind. Many consider the Ten Commandments to

---

[247] Other cases contemplated in the Code of Hammurabi include a son striking his father, which allowed cutting off his hands as punishment (Law 195). A free man putting out the eye of the son of another free man, which allowed the aggressor's own eye to be put out in return (Law 196). And a man breaking the bone of another man, for which the aggressor's bone would be broken (Law 197).

be universally applicable, that is, natural law, always in force regardless of the law in force, or positive law.

Other materials used to issue legal rules have been papyrus, mainly in Egypt since about 3000 BC[248]; clay tablets used in ancient Mesopotamia since about 3200 BC[249]; and parchment, made of animal skin, especially goat, sheep, or calf, used in antiquity and the Middle Ages.

In the era before the Internet Revolution, rules were written primarily on paper[250]. Since the discovery of the printing press by Johannes Gutenberg in the 1440s, paper has been the dominant medium for publishing legal rules. The printing press is widely considered one of the most important inventions in human history because it revolutionized the dissemination of knowledge and facilitated the

---

[248] The ancient Egyptians developed a technique for making papyrus sheets from the Cyperus papyrus plant, which grew on the banks of the Nile River. The plant was cut into strips and woven into sheets to form a scroll on which to write extensively for administrative, literary, and religious documents. It became one of the principal means of writing in the ancient world. The production and use of papyrus continued well into Roman times, when it was replaced by parchment and later paper.

[249] The inhabitants of ancient Mesopotamia used clay tablets for cuneiform writing, one of the oldest writing systems in the world. These tablets were used for a variety of purposes, including accounting, administrative records, laws, correspondence, and literary and religious texts. Clay could be molded into tablets and written on with a stylus. The tablets were then dried in the sun or fired to harden them, ensuring durability.

[250] Paper was invented in China around the 2nd century A.D. and became widely used throughout the world after the Arabs introduced it to Europe in the 8th century. It was originally made from shredded plant fibers that were pressed into sheets.

propagation of ideas through the mass reproduction of texts.

The most relevant legal norm of the Industrial Revolution was the Napoleonic Civil Code of 1804. Regulation through a single unifying code followed the patterns of the Industrial Revolution mentioned in *Chapter 2: Centralization, Standardization, Synchronization, and Massification*. The Civil Code unified into a single coherent and accessible body a legal system that had been fragmented by different laws across different regions of France.

The Code also legally consolidated one of the characteristic principles of the French Revolution, namely the equality of the masses. Privileges were eliminated, and ecclesiastical regulation was repealed. The pillars of the Middle Ages were annihilated.

The only true equality of the human being was eliminated in the French Revolution: an original equality based on the same nature and dignity[251]. This equality is compatible with the uniqueness of each human being, because each person is unique. This is why each person develops individual capacities, so that some are more intelligent or capable than others. Some qualities are more valued than others by society as a whole.

As Ulpian pointed out, justice is giving to each his own. Our modern decadent state eliminated original

---

[251] I recommend reading St. John Paul II's Theology of the Body, which explores this idea in depth.

natural equality and established an unreal social equality. This occurred in both communist and democratic countries, in the former more overtly, in the latter gradually through an increase in control. The problem of false equality is not merely political, but epochal. In the end, it is the state, communist, socialist, or democratic, that decides what to give to each person under the principle of social justice, by virtue of which all must be equal.

The principle of equality has been an idealistic mirage that guided the masses during the Industrial Revolution, together with the bureaucratic machinery of the modern state. George Orwell captured this in Animal Farm. The rule of the animal society was that all animals are equal. But then it evolved into all animals are equal, but some animals are more equal than others.

Elites guided and directed the masses, and continue to do so today, in both communist and democratic countries. The apparent, false, and superficial equality created by the modern state will be unmasked by the Internet Revolution, in which the individual will regain his differentiating status in the world.

The ideas of equality and legal unification were disseminated throughout Europe during Napoleon's conquests. The Code was introduced in several European countries, including Italy, the Netherlands, Belgium, parts of Germany, and Poland. Many countries adopted the Napoleonic Code into their own legal systems.

For example, the German Civil Code (BGB) and the Italian Civil Code were influenced by the Napoleonic Code. After the wars of independence in Latin America, many new states adopted the Napoleonic Code or legal systems inspired by it, such as Mexico, Brazil, and Chile.

Most contrary to the Napoleonic Code are the digital laws emanating from the Internet Revolution. Like an immense block of ice, regulatory centralization will melt in favor of the decentralization of law. Blockchain technology and digital assets allow anyone to issue digital laws from anywhere in the world in a horizontal way, consistent with the Internet, rather than a vertical way, consistent with the state.

Before the emergence of digital laws, the idea that code is law was developed in the 1990s. The World Wide Web laid the foundation for the expansion and popularization of the Internet as we know it today[252]. In the 1990s, several voices advanced the idea that code is law. The growth in computer and Internet use led to the proliferation of software programs that users could adopt or reject. Through software, the programmer becomes a legislator. He can specify what a user may or may not do in a given environment, often more

---

[252] The World Wide Web (www) was invented by British scientist Tim Berners-Lee in 1989. In 1990, Berners-Lee wrote the first web browser, the first web server, and the first web pages, establishing the foundations of the World Wide Web.

effectively than the traditional legislator. In short, the coder regulates behaviors that shape people's lives. This is what Joel Reidenberg described as lex informatica in 1992. The concept was later popularized as code is law by Lawrence Lessig.[253,254]

Finally, since the issuance of Bitcoin, we can confirm the existence of digital laws. Unlike code is law, digital laws can produce simultaneous and instantaneous effects across multiple parts of the world. The Internet community has already regulated deflationary currencies such as Bitcoin and Litecoin; digital laws that facilitate the efficient issuance of other digital currencies, such as Ethereum, Solana, BNB Smart Chain, and Polygon; stablecoins such as USDT; and decentralized exchanges of digital assets without trusted third parties, such as Uniswap, PancakeSwap, and SushiSwap.

This is only the beginning of a new form of social and legal organization. As the community grows and the market matures, digital laws will regulate other aspects of a society that is increasingly digital, and that will become further digitized as the Internet Revolution unfolds.

---

[253] De Filippi, Primavera, and Samer Hassan. (2016). Blockchain Technology as a Regulatory Technology: From "Code is Law" to "Law is Code." First Monday. hal-01676880.

[254] Lawrence Lessig develops this idea in his book Code and Other Laws of Cyberspace (1999).

3. Law and Society or Law and Community

From a legal point of view, the first question is whether digital laws can be considered law in the strict sense.

Christian Thomasius' thesis is that outside society, there is no law, and in every society, there is law[255]. Law and society are mutually and necessarily required, so there can be no law without society, nor can there be society without law. They are reversible concepts in the sense that, if we encounter one and turn it around, we find the other. They are two sides of the same coin.

Let us not forget that it is society, not the state, that is the creator and bearer of law. A widespread trend today, typical of a paternalistic state, is to assume that only the state can create law. According to this thesis, it would not be possible to issue a digital law such as Bitcoin. The falsity of that thesis was already explained in Chapter 1. Bitcoin is a digital law that operates in a non-state jurisdiction, the Internet, that was issued privately, and that exercises its effects through a blockchain.

If digital laws are recognized as law, the decisive criterion is not who promulgates them, but whether the community treats the rule set as binding, relies on it in practice, and organizes behavior around the predictability of its outcomes. In that sense, protocols

[255] "Extra societatem non est ius, in omni societate ius est."

can function as institutions, and institutions can exist without territorial borders.

It is worth remembering that society endorses the political organization of the state, not the other way around. For most of our history, mankind was organized without states, which were created, as we conceive them today, in the 17th century. The first human societies appeared more than 100,000 years ago.

In short, society creates the law and will continue to create it as it wishes and can, according to the technique at its disposal. In any case, if we confirm the existence of a digital society, we confirm the existence of digital law and therefore digital laws. In this new digital society, speed, security, and efficiency in transmitting and storing information stand out. In the new network, localism, nationalism, and bureaucracy have little value. The national citizen born of the French Revolution will fade, and the private individual will reemerge.

Before the Internet, society was made up of a group of people. After the Internet, it becomes a community. That is why on the Internet, we are not looking for a society with its law, but a community with its law.

There is no doubt that the community related to blockchain technology is growing. In Chapter 1, I noted that, using data from 2023, it is estimated that about

420 million people hold bitcoin[256]. There are currently more bitcoin holders than basketball players in the world. I also noted that about 2.5 million digital laws, or cryptoassets, have been issued[257].

Cryptoassets are deposited in electronic wallets, and the number of wallets is also increasing. Coin98 Analytics reported that the number of wallet addresses at the end of 2023[258] was 1.8 billion, almost double the number at the beginning of the year, when it counted 914 million addresses.

While one person may control several wallets or addresses, the data still reflects a clear increase in sector activity, and therefore in its community.

From the standpoint of wallet activity, the most active blockchain in 2023 was BNB Chain (BSC). In terms of unique addresses, BSC closed the year with 413.7 million addresses, according to metrics from BscScan[259]. That represents a 74% increase over the 236 million addresses recorded in January. During 2023, BNB Chain recorded a record 36.2 million-plus

---

[256] Criptonoticias. (January 19, 2023). Número de usuarios de Bitcoin y criptomonedas creció 40% en 2022: reporte. Accessed October 23, 2023 from https://www.criptonoticias.com/comunidad/adopcion/numero-usuarios-bitcoin-criptomonedas-crecio-40-2022-reporte/

[257] Daly, L. (August 19, 2024). How many cryptocurrencies are there? The Motley Fool. Accessed March 6, 2024, from https://www.fool.com/investing/stock-market/market-sectors/financials/cryptocurrency-stocks/how-many-cryptocurrencies-are-there/

[258] Coin98 Analytics. (January 1, 2024). X post on wallet addresses. Source: https://x.com/Coin98Analytics/status/1742104162555535486

[259] BscScan. Chart of unique addresses. https://bscscan.com/chart/address

transactions on December 7, according to Artemis data. Despite losing prominence, BNB Chain stood out as the leading blockchain for decentralized finance (DeFi) during 2023[260].

Polygon is a blockchain that aims to improve the scalability of Ethereum. It had the highest address growth in 2023, adding more than 185.9 million. Polygon went from 206 million unique addresses in January to 392.3 million by the end of 2023, according to metrics from Polygonscan[261], which implies an annual growth of 90%.

In global terms, the largest communities are Bitcoin, with a market dominance of 50%, and Ethereum, with a dominance of 20%.

Perhaps the most interesting protocol from a community point of view is Ethereum. It is the largest blockchain infrastructure for creating decentralized applications in the industry. In 2023, it increased its number of unique addresses by 16%, according to Coin98 Analytics. On an annual basis, Ethereum's addresses went from 218.5 million recorded in January to about 254 million recorded in December, according to figures from Etherscan[262]. In other words, Ethereum

---

260 González, D. J. (January 4, 2024). Descubre las 5 blockchains que tuvieron más usuarios en 2023. Observatorio Blockchain. Accessed June 5, 2024 from https://observatorioblockchain.com/blockchain/descubre-las-5-blockchains-que-tuvieron-mas-usuarios-en-2023/

261 Polygonscan. Chart of unique addresses https://polygonscan.com/chart/address

262 Etherscan. Chart of unique addresses. https://etherscan.io/chart/address

registered more than 35 million new addresses in 2023.

The analysis of wallet creation gives us a clue to activity on a blockchain. But the community is not made up only of holders, or hodlers in crypto terminology.

The Ethereum community can be accessed from its own website[263]. One might assume that Ethereum is made up only of committed holders of the cryptoasset. Nothing could be further from the truth. Ethereum includes hundreds of thousands of developers, technologists, designers, users, holders, and enthusiasts.

On Ethereum, anyone can submit proposals for protocol improvements, known as Ethereum Improvement Proposals, or EIPs. EIPs are digital law reform proposals submitted by the community for review and potential adoption. They may include standards that specify new features or processes for Ethereum. EIPs contain technical specifications for proposed changes and act as an authoritative source for the community. Network upgrades and application standards are discussed and developed through the established EIP process[264].

Viewed this way, community governance becomes a legislative workflow. Proposals compete, attract support, undergo technical review, and then, if

---

[263] Ethereum Foundation. Community page. https://ethereum.org/es/community/

[264] Ethereum. (July 14, 2024). Introduction to Ethereum Improvement Proposals (EIP). Accessed September 6, 2024, from https://ethereum.org/es/eips/

adopted, become binding through implementation. The process is public by default, and the legitimacy of the rule change depends on transparency and broad participation rather than on formal state authority.

Ethereum is a good example of how new forms of regulation and organization in society are being born in a decentralized way. Francis Sanchinelli is one of the founders of Ethereum Guatemala. He has been part of the Ethereum community in Latin America since 2022 and has actively participated in regional communities. He has also organized the ETH LATAM event, the largest community gathering in Latin America.

For Sanchinelli, the Ethereum community is focused on solving problems using blockchain technology and smart contracts. What matters is that the organization of the community is decentralized and promotes collaboration through networking and face-to-face events. It is easy to become part of the Ethereum community through established groups. The idea is that anyone can form and drive communities. In addition, leaders in the region are accessible for sharing learning and best practices.

Sanchinelli believes that the Ethereum community differs substantially from the Bitcoin community. Ethereum is more focused on technology and how to contribute to society. In contrast, the Bitcoin community is more focused on Bitcoin's role as a store of value and its function as money. The truth is that Bitcoin and Ethereum are complementary.

Like Ethereum and Bitcoin, other protocols also have communities that support them. Similar models exist in other proposals such as Cardano, Solana, Polkadot, Tron, and others.

4. Legal Characteristics of Digital Laws

Digital Laws arising in Internet jurisdiction, such as Bitcoin, Ethereum, and other cryptoassets, operate as private law. They are self-regulating, digital, difficult to override in practice, and often self-executing once the relevant conditions are met.

Put differently, a Digital Law is a rule-set embedded in open-source code, validated by a distributed network, and enforced through consensus and incentives rather than through a state monopoly on coercion.

4.1. Private law

Digital Laws are private laws arising from the community, much like the historical emergence of commercial law. From a historical perspective, the most effective law has often been private ordering rather than public command. This is the thesis Bruce L. Benson develops in his book The Enterprise of Law: Justice Without the State.

For Benson, modern reliance on government to create laws and establish order has not been the general rule, at least historically. For example, public police services were not imposed in the United States and Great Britain until the middle of the 19th century, and they faced resistance from citizens[265]. Similarly,

[265] Benson, Bruce L. (2011). The Enterprise of Law: Justice without the State. Introduction. Oakland, California. Kindle edition.

commercial law, like many Digital Laws, was created by merchants themselves rather than by a centralized state authority. Benson also notes that a large share of commercial disputes in the United States are resolved through private dispute-resolution mechanisms such as arbitration, not by public bodies[266].

Historically, laws can be issued from above by a higher authority such as a king, legislator, or supreme court. But laws can also arise from below, that is, from society itself. The best example of law born from below is custom, created through repeated practice and broad acceptance. Law imposed from above relies on minority power and usually requires more force to ensure compliance. Law born from below relies on mutual recognition and voluntary adherence.

Digital Laws do not emanate from above through a central authority. They emerge from the base of society, which in the Internet era is better described as a community. Digital Laws require broad acceptance. Otherwise, even if the code is live and the protocol is technically "in force," it will have little practical sovereignty because few people rely on it[267].

Unlike custom, Digital Laws do not need years of repeated practice before they can operate. The technique allows a Digital Law to be issued directly. Once it operates in an Internet jurisdiction, the

---

266 Idem.

267 Idem.

community may adopt it, reject it, or improve it through upgrades or competing protocols.

The key point about private law born from below is that it is wanted by the community because participants recognize benefits and share expectations[268]. Bitcoin generates the expectation that its payment system will work, that it is auditable, and that its monetary policy is highly resistant to discretionary change. Ethereum generates the expectation that it can serve as infrastructure for issuing and operating additional Digital Laws through smart contracts. These expectations are accepted, valued, and implemented by the community.

Hayek's horizontal view of law is also relevant here. What matters are reasonably foreseeable expectations that correspond to practices on which the daily conduct of group members is based. Those expectations guide behavior. Practices that everyone expects to be honored, and that condition the success of most activities, come to be treated as binding[269]. In the case of Digital Laws, these expectations are codified. Instead of custom turning into law after repeated practice, the law is written in code and then either adopted or rejected in practice.

---

[268] Benson, Bruce L. (2011). The Enterprise of Law: Justice Without the State. Introduction. Oakland, California. Kindle edition.

[269] Hayek, F. A. (1973). Law, Legislation and Liberty, vol. 1: Rules and Order (pp. 96–97). University of Chicago Press.

Private customary rules are often based on reciprocity. Parties recognize a duty to follow the rule because doing so benefits them and the group. Punishment is typically imposed from above, but incentives are often the foundation of private customary law[270]. Incentives are central to Bitcoin because those who support the network can receive rewards, and the broader community understands why those incentives matter for security. Incentive design is also a foundation of decentralized finance, which I will address later when discussing Uniswap and similar protocols.

Fuller suggests three conditions for a private obligation to be clear and broadly accepted. First, reciprocity, where the obligation arises from a voluntary agreement by the parties. Second, performance of reciprocal obligations of comparable value. Third, a relationship with society that remains stable enough that what binds one person today will also bind third parties today and tomorrow. In other words, obligations are reversible[271].

Private dispute resolution mattered at the birth of commercial law and will be equally relevant in digital law. An arbitrator applies the rules to resolve disputes and, through repeated decisions, can clarify or develop

---

[270] Idem.

[271] Fuller, L. L. (1977). The Morality of Law (pp. 23–24). Yale University Press.

new rules that emerge from practice[272]. That is why specialized arbitration institutions, such as those offered by Blockchain Arbitration and Commerce Society (BACS), can play a meaningful role for communities that transact under Internet-native rules[273].

A core principle of commercial law is party autonomy, the freedom to adopt agreements and bind oneself. Blockchain technology is creating a new technical architecture for commerce. Contracts will increasingly be natively digital, including tokenized instruments recorded on an immutable ledger. Execution can be automated through smart contracts. Where real-world performance is involved, the architecture can still reduce enforcement costs by automating the on-chain parts and clarifying what must happen off-chain to complete the bargain.

4.2. Self-regulating law

As I noted in Chapter 1, Bitcoin is self-regulating. It did not emanate from states or governments. Bitcoin's codified, programmed regulation was made available to the community.

Bitcoin and other cryptocurrencies contain their core operating rules in code. This technically enabled

---

[272] Hayek, F. A. (1973). Law, Legislation and Liberty, vol. 1: Rules and Order (p. 99). University of Chicago Press.

[273] Blockchain Arbitration and Commerce Society (BACS). https://bacsociety.com/

approach represents a break with centuries of centralized legal organization.

The door Bitcoin opens is the possibility of regulating key economic relationships without state bureaucracy, in a more transparent, efficient, and cost-effective way.

As private law arising from a social base, Digital Laws belong to the community. The community decides the future of a given Digital Law because it believes that using it produces both individual and collective benefits. That benefit must be fair, balanced, and reciprocal if the rule is to survive in the long run.

The community can propose minor changes and improvements. Some are accepted and integrated; others are not. When a large part of the community rejects a proposed change but another part adopts it, a split can occur so that two Digital Laws emerge from one. This is called a hard fork.

A clear example occurred with The DAO, a decentralized organization on the Ethereum network. It suffered an attack on June 16, 2016, in which unknown hackers stole about 3.6 million ether, roughly $50 million at the time[274]. Because of The DAO's design, funds could not be withdrawn for 28 days, which created time for the community to respond.

---

[274] https://estrategiasdeinversion.com (February 18, 2022). Ethereum Classic: el hard fork tras la crisis de "The DAO". Accessed August 30, 2024, from https://www.estrategiasdeinversion.com/actualidad/noticias/bolsa-eeuu/ethereum-classic-el-hard-fork-tras-la-crisis-de-n-504697

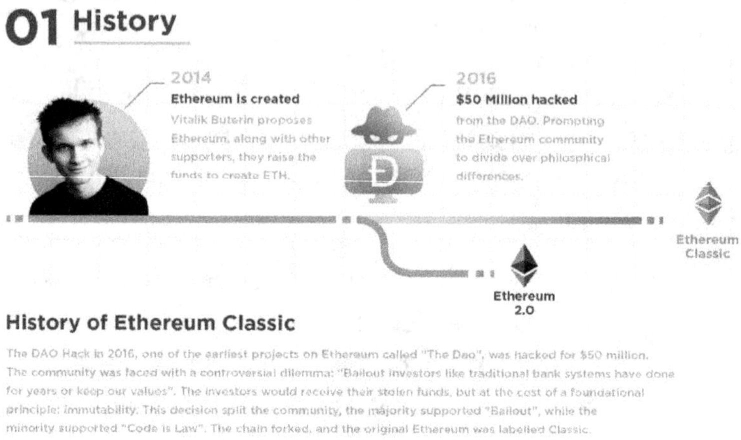

Fig. 13. Source: estrategiasdeinversion.com

Ethereum founder Vitalik Buterin proposed a soft fork to identify the attacker and prevent access to the stolen funds. A soft fork does not create two networks. It keeps one chain but changes how certain transactions are treated, in this case by preventing the attack transaction from being processed.

The attacker responded that his actions were "legal" because the vulnerability existed in The DAO's code. He threatened legal action and even offered bounties for those who refused to follow the proposed soft fork.

The community faced a moral and legal dilemma: can an "immutable" ledger be changed to undo a harmful transaction? The community chose a hard fork, rolling back the Ethereum network's state to a point before the DAO attack. For some, this violated the principle of immutability and created a precedent that could undermine trust in the protocol.

On July 20, 2016, the hard fork was implemented at block 1,920,000. Since then, two Digital Laws have coexisted: Ethereum and Ethereum Classic.[275]

This episode shows that "self-regulation" is not only technical. Code constrains behavior, but legitimacy is supplied by the people and institutions that decide which chain they recognize as authoritative.

4.3. Digital or virtual law

Bitcoin and other cryptocurrencies are Internet-native law. They can be called Digital Laws operating in Internet jurisdiction. Rules issued by states and merely published on the Internet are not Digital Laws. They are digitized rules.

Digital Laws operate through open-source software available online, and their normative effects are sealed through a blockchain's consensus process. Bitcoin is Internet money. It deploys its effects on the Internet and from the Internet. In the same way, the rules that govern Bitcoin are Internet norms that operate on the Internet and through the Internet.

Over time, many rights will be represented through tokens or other cryptoassets linked to a blockchain.

---

[275] Liquidity-provider.com. (February 13, 2024). ¿Qué era La DAO? La Historia del Infame Hackeo. Accessed August 30, 2024, from https://liquidity-provider.com/es/articles/what-was-the-dao-the-story-of-infamous-hack/

Tokenization has several advantages. First, rights can be transferred globally with speed and low cost. Second, many intermediaries required by state-based systems become optional or unnecessary. Third, when obligations are defined in code, enforcement can occur automatically for the on-chain parts of the deal, which increases practical effectiveness.

The main challenge is the bridge between traditional registry systems and blockchain-based registries. Tokenization of serious legal business requires reliable connections to real-world facts, including identity, capacity, and the existence of collateral. Those connections may be created through contractual wrappers, regulated custodians, and trustworthy oracles, but they must be designed carefully to avoid reintroducing the very weaknesses the blockchain sought to remove.

As the community matures, it will be able to offer tokenizations with stronger guarantees for the parties and for society at large. Waiting passively for state regulation is a mistake if the community can build workable standards first. At the same time, some rights, especially those involving physical assets, will continue to depend on off-chain enforcement and public institutions until bridging mechanisms become widely recognized.

4.4. Non-derogable law

The regulation of a Digital Law can be more resistant to unilateral change than state law. This is one reason we can speak of Internet jurisdiction operating de facto alongside state regulation.

Each Digital Law defines how it can be modified by the community. In Bitcoin, changes are proposed through Bitcoin Improvement Proposals (BIPs).[276] In Ethereum, proposals are called Ethereum Improvement Proposals (EIPs).[277, 278]

Bitcoin's core rules include the cap of 21 million bitcoins and the projected final issuance around the year 2140. These essential rules can be changed only if a sufficient share of the network adopts a compatible change. In practice, changing them would risk the protocol's credibility, which is why trivial amendments to monetary policy are unlikely.

This strength is not absolute. States can still regulate people and institutions at the edges, such as exchanges, custodians, and tax-reporting channels. But at the protocol level, the rule-set is difficult to

---

[276] I address this issue below when explaining the Bitcoin Digital Law. Specifically, I attach as Annex 1 to this work a regulation of Bitcoin in traditional format that includes this type of change in its Article 9.

[277] Pirus, B. (July 9, 2020). Ripple partners with Santander for international payments. Cointelegraph. Accessed March 11, 2024, from https://es.cointelegraph.com/news/ripple-teams-up-with-santander-on-international-payments

[278] I address this issue below when explaining the Ethereum Digital Law. Specifically, I attach as Annex 2 to this work a regulation of Ethereum in traditional format that includes this type of change in its Article 8.

override without broad, voluntary coordination across the network. That is a new kind of legal resilience.

There can also be drawbacks. Ethereum changed its consensus mechanism from proof of work (PoW) to proof of stake (PoS). The change required broad support across the ecosystem and took years of preparation. Some miners objected and proposed alternative chains, including EthereumPoW (ETHW), which still uses PoW. The switch to PoS was widely supported by other participants and ultimately succeeded after a long transition.

Bitcoin.org has addressed a related question: could users conspire against Bitcoin? The answer reflects the reality that hostile coordination is constrained by incentives, transparency, and the need for broad agreement to sustain a harmful change.[279]

4.5. Executive law

Digital Laws are programmed executive laws. They are codified rules that can be enforced through the protocol. Generally, a Digital Law contains both dispositive and executive rules. Dispositive rules describe what the parties agree to. Executive rules determine what happens when the agreed conditions are met.

Here lies one of the great advantages of Digital Laws: they include mechanisms that facilitate

---

[279] Bitcoin.org. (n.d.). ¿Podrían los usuarios conspirar contra Bitcoin? Accessed September 7, 2024, from https://bitcoin.org/es/faq#podrian-los-usuarios-conspirar-en-contra-de-bitcoin

normative self-execution without traditional intermediaries.

Satoshi Nakamoto, in his white paper, created an electronic cash system without relying on a financial institution.[280] But the impact goes beyond bypassing banks. Rules passed in parliaments require executive and judicial institutions to ensure compliance. Digital Laws often execute directly: once a transaction is voluntarily initiated and validated, it becomes part of a block that the network treats as final.

Self-execution is strongest where the entire performance occurs on-chain. Where a transaction depends on real-world facts, enforcement still benefits from clear, automated escrow, collateral management, and auditability, but it may still require external evidence and dispute resolution to connect the chain to reality.

This system of executive rights can include issuing currency, representing rights in tokens, exchanging assets, collateralized lending, interest payments for deposits, and many other products that will emerge as the community grows.

---

280 Satoshi Nakamoto. (2008). Bitcoin: A Peer-to-Peer Electronic Cash System. https://bitcoin.org/bitcoin.pdf

5. The Separation of Powers in Internet Jurisdiction

The separation of powers in the Modern State[281], as a constitutional idea, differs from governance in the Internet Revolution. In a centralized system of government, separating legislative, executive, and judicial power is meant to prevent abuse and protect rights.

The legislative branch creates, modifies, and repeals laws. It typically operates through parliaments, congresses, or legislative assemblies.

The executive branch enforces the laws, administers the government, and directs national and international policy. It is composed of a head of state and a head of government, along with ministers and officials who form the cabinet.

The judiciary resolves disputes and aims to apply the law fairly and impartially through courts and judges.

In Internet jurisdiction, there is no single institution that must be restrained by a formal separation of powers. The system is decentralized. No parliament is required because adoption is voluntary and distributed: a user's choice of software and a node operator's choice of rules can be enough.

---

[281] As developed by Montesquieu in The Spirit of the Laws, published in 1748.

Even so, a functional separation often emerges. Developers and researchers propose changes, node operators and validators enforce the active rule-set, and dispute resolution can be handled by arbitration forums, reputational systems, or protocol-level mechanisms. The roles differ, and that diversity can reduce single points of failure.

The democratic system of the Modern State does not guarantee that the best rules are those approved by parliaments. Many states exhibit hyper-regulation: numerous ineffective rules that can be detrimental to growth, as some critics argue is the case in parts of the European Union.

Internet jurisdiction also does not require trusted third parties, such as political parties, general elections, or bills submitted for parliamentary approval. The decentralized system is simpler. A Digital Law is written in code and published to the Internet jurisdiction. The community then freely chooses whether to use it, giving it practical validity.

Unlike state law, which is typically of mandatory application within a territory, Internet jurisdiction is closer to right a la carte: individuals and organizations choose among competing rule-sets. Digital hyper-regulation is self-defeating because a protocol that fails to deliver value will be abandoned.

For example, a person might choose Bitcoin as a deflationary savings protocol, Ethereum as infrastructure for tokenized instruments, Polygon for faster and cheaper applications as a layer 2 for

Ethereum, or XRP because of its banking-oriented ecosystem. The point is that selection is voluntary and market-like.

Likewise, the Internet Revolution is breaking down the old wall between a few lawmakers and the many who must follow their rules. Digital Laws make it possible for the same person to be both a rule-maker and a rule-user, issuing new Digital Laws while freely adopting others that match their interests and expertise.

The executive or decentralized governance power in Internet jurisdiction is often described through DAOs (decentralized autonomous organizations). DAOs emerged after the development of Ethereum-based smart contracts. They operate through code on a blockchain and can resemble trading companies, cooperatives, or community property arrangements known in state jurisdictions.[282] Some state jurisdictions

---

[282] DAOs use blockchain technology to manage and execute operations without a centralized authority. They rely on smart contracts, self-executing computer programs that define the organization's rules and procedures. Smart contracts are written in code and execute automatically when predefined conditions are met. Members of a DAO can interact with the organization and vote on decisions using tokens or cryptocurrencies associated with the DAO. DAOs have been used for a variety of purposes, including managing investment funds, democratic decision-making in decentralized communities, and coordinating collaborative online projects. Some DAOs are fully autonomous, while others combine automation with human governance.

recognize legal effects of DAOs in limited ways, including Utah[283] and Wyoming.[284]

Finally, the judicial power of the Internet Revolution is still developing. As legal transactions become tokenized, many will execute on-chain without traditional intermediaries. State courts may be complemented or displaced by faster conflict-resolution systems. In this model, arbitrators and courts can act as legal oracles by introducing authoritative data, such as an award, into a system that can execute the result on-chain.

Submission to one dispute-resolution system or another will be chosen by sovereign individuals and firms. Those who value speed and effectiveness will choose the systems that deliver it. Those who wish to avoid obligations will often try to remain in the slower, more bureaucratic channels of the legacy system.

Private judges and community-based arbitrators will increasingly resolve disputes arising under Internet-native rules, especially where the dispute can be remedied through on-chain execution.

---

[283] Nwaokocha, A. (March 7, 2023). Las DAO obtienen reconocimiento legal en EE.UU. gracias a la aprobación de la Ley DAO de Utah. Cointelegraph. Accessed March 7, 2024, from https://es.cointelegraph.com/news/dao-gets-legal-recognition-in-the-us-as-the-utah-dao-act-passess

[284] Pereira, A. P. (March 8, 2024). Wyoming aprueba ley otorgando estatus legal a las DAOs. Cointelegraph. Accessed March 15, 2024, from https://es.cointelegraph.com/news/wyoming-passes-law-granting-dao-legal-status

6. The New Legal System of the Internet Revolution

I mentioned in Chapter 2 that great revolutions are often recognized only after years, or even centuries. There is still time for the issuance of Digital Laws to become as ordinary as watching videos on YouTube or shopping online. The shift is not only technological. It is institutional because it changes how people coordinate trust, property, and enforcement across borders.

In the coming years, a growing share of the world's assets will be represented as tokens, transferred via blockchains, and held in wallets. Not every asset will move on-chain at the same speed, but the direction is clear: the infrastructure for digitized ownership is being built in public.

Transmitting shares of a trading company to anyone in the world can become faster and safer than buying a product on Amazon. Settlement can move from days to minutes, with an audit trail that is visible to participants and regulators alike.

It should be noted that we are still in the first phase of this disruptive market, characterized by speculation, uneven quality, and rapid experimentation. What happened with early equity markets, commodity cycles, and metals is being repeated today with cryptoassets. To dismiss this emerging market as a mere bubble with no future, as much mainstream commentary still suggests, is to misdiagnose.

Speculation is not the same as utility. Speculation often arrives first because markets can price expectations long before real-world workflows migrate. The legal and commercial question is which Digital Laws convert attention into durable, repeatable use.

The cryptoasset market of the 21st century is similar to the market for mercantile shares of the 18th century. Many investments of that time were a real fiasco, just as many investments in cryptoassets are today. For example, the South Sea Company, founded in England in 1711, promised huge profits, which attracted many investors. It seemed a safe bet, given that it received a monopoly on trade with South America.

In 1720, the company's stock skyrocketed due to rampant speculation and misleading promotional tactics. However, when it became clear that the promises of profits were exaggerated and would not be fulfilled, the bubble burst. Stock prices plummeted, causing financial ruin for many investors. The same happened with the Mississippi Company in France, and the same can be said of many speculative crypto projects.

These collapses resulted in a loss of confidence in the market. They also prompted reforms intended to regulate financial markets and prevent similar frauds in the future. In practice, early failures forced the development of basic guardrails, such as clearer disclosure, better custody, and stronger standards for identifying misconduct.

According to 2021 data, global market capitalization was about $31.7 trillion[285]. New markets cannot be scorned because of the failures, misleading actions, and collapses of their initial stage. The Internet, blockchains, and cryptocurrencies will be adopted faster than public equities were. Just look at the impact the Internet has had since the late 1990s. Network effects compound quickly once the tools become simple enough for ordinary users.

The gold business did not get off to a good start either. In its beginnings, it suffered economic bubbles similar to those we are witnessing today with cryptoassets. In the United States, there was the California gold rush (1848–1855), and in Canada, the Klondike gold rush (1896–1899). Many of those who went in search of wealth found ruin. A similar story can be told by many investors in cryptoassets. Yet gold did not cease to weigh the economy, eventually becoming the monetary standard for state-issued currencies until governments abandoned that model in the 20th century.

For those of us witnessing the birth of digital law, the difficulty lies in separating the wheat from the chaff: finding the Digital Laws that truly bring value, and then

---

[285] Sobrino, C. (n.d.). Global Top 100 companies by market capitalisation. PwC. Accessed July 22, 2024, from https://www.pwc.es/es/publicaciones/auditoria/global-top-100-companies-2021-markets-capitalisation.html

understanding why, regardless of the speculation inherent in any investment. A useful test is whether a protocol earns trust through transparent rules, credible decentralization, and security that is costly to attack.

Bitcoin, Ethereum, and many other protocols provide value. At the same time, a very high percentage of Digital Laws, or cryptoassets, are born for purely speculative purposes, without providing the market with a real product or practical utility. They become mere bets that are easy to create and manage with new technologies, looking for speculative investors to play with. In fact, some of these Digital Laws have been labeled by the community itself as "shitcoins," that is, worthless currencies. Investing in these assets can feel like going to the casino. If the only promise is price appreciation, there is rarely a durable legal or economic function underneath.

In a society crowded with fake news, radical opinions, and information manipulation, it is difficult to identify which Digital Laws are or are not important.

Bitcoin, for example, has been repeatedly compared by mainstream commentary to the Tulip Bubble (1636–1637). Tulip bulbs became an object of investment, and prices soared to astronomical levels. In 1637, tulip prices fell sharply, causing huge losses to investors who had bought bulbs at inflated prices. The Tulip Bubble is one of the earliest examples of a speculative bubble and market collapse, highlighting the dangers of unbridled speculation. But the asset "tulip" differs completely from the asset "bitcoin." Tulips were scarce objects whose price was driven by fashion. Bitcoin is a bearer digital asset with a fixed issuance schedule that can be verified by anyone running the software. Bitcoin continues to rise in value over the long term, something that did not happen with tulips. This misleading comparison shows how institutions and pundits insist that we do not understand Bitcoin.

The Tulip Bubble is more comparable to the NFT fad, or to other cryptocurrencies that do not contribute anything of value. They were issued with hype, attracted investors, and later saw their value fall with corresponding losses.

Both Bitcoin and Ethereum are among the most relevant Digital Laws of the free, horizontal, and decentralized Internet system. It is no coincidence that BlackRock and other large funds have focused exchange-traded funds on Bitcoin and Ethereum[286], not on short-lived speculative projects. Institutional interest tends to cluster around assets with clearer rules, deeper liquidity, and stronger security.

In the early stage of the cryptoasset market we are witnessing, and as once happened with stock markets and gold, the presence of manipulators and low-quality Digital Laws is not alarming. It is typical of a community

---

[286] These are exchange-traded funds that track the price of Bitcoin and Ethereum, allowing investors to gain exposure to these cryptocurrencies without having to buy and store them directly.

that has just been born. As the market matures, the community will adopt measures that increase quality.

As with commercial law, it is up to the community to create new institutions, associations, or guilds consistent with the principles of the Internet Revolution. That includes standards bodies, auditors, reputation systems, and specialized arbitration forums that can resolve disputes quickly and transparently without collapsing back into state bureaucracy. As the sovereign community grows, states will lose power, control, and strength.

Time will play in favor of the Internet Revolution. Once the initial phase is over, more practical applications will emerge in Internet Jurisdiction, and more realities of ordinary life will be executed with the advantages of this technology. For many people born before 1989, understanding Bitcoin can feel as complex as solving a Rubik's Cube; for Generation Z and "Generation Bitcoin," investing in cryptoassets, using a wallet, buying Bitcoin, or choosing a blockchain can become as commonplace as reading the printed newspaper once was.

In the new community, citizens will cease to be mere citizens and will become aware that they are "sovereign individuals"[287]. Just as new generations will not understand life in a non-digital world, sovereign individuals will not understand solutions offered by

---

[287] The concept "sovereign individual" is developed by William Rees-Mogg and James Dale Davidson in The Sovereign Individual.

outdated institutions. For them, voting in a general election will not feel decisive. Instead, which digital asset to use for day-to-day payments, or which crypto-association to join for business, will be more important.

This second phase of Internet Jurisdiction will be stronger because the community will be larger, and it will understand that it is the community, not states, that must regulate and function in this system without trusted third parties. The principle of decentralization, fundamental at first to survive state hostility, will evolve into a community that is confident in living under a new, Internet-native legal order.

To be, or not to be, a national of a country will no longer imply a moral burden. Sovereign individuals will choose residence, and later nationality, by virtue of fiscal, commercial, and personal advantages.

It is in this phase of maturity that the new law emanating from Digital Laws will flourish. Gradually, the economy, goods, and rights will be tokenized. In short, a significant part of the economy will be tokenized. The reason is simple: the new legal system for doing business will be among the most effective, cheapest, fastest, and most transparent ever created.

In this phase, as economic life becomes increasingly digitized on blockchains, traditional institutions born in the Industrial Revolution will gradually fall into disuse. The social contract, like a leaky bellows, will lose strength until it is effectively repealed by the Internet Revolution. Governments, accustomed to interfering in civil life, will not be able to stop the issuance of Internet Digital Laws. Institutions that do not adapt will be as decorative as an encyclopedia gathering dust in a living room.

The big change will occur first in the commercial sphere, which will revolve around a new legal system formed by blockchain infrastructure and the Digital Laws of the Internet. This system will succeed because of practicality, structural cost savings, reduction of intermediaries, and efficiency in solving problems. Digital Law will force rulers to compete by offering services that people actually want, rather than rules that merely expand bureaucracy.

Digital Laws will be so successful that they will force rulers to think about their subjects for the first time in many years. They will have no choice but to issue rules that help people's practical lives. Politics will be regenerated. The self-centered profile of many of today's politicians will have less incentive to enter politics, because the system will offer fewer opportunities for personal profit.

A new commercial law will emerge. Trading companies will be created directly and in a decentralized way, on a blockchain. The community will accept these companies as valid, and therefore their agreements will be binding. In many cases, these entities will resemble DAOs or tokenized corporations whose governance rules are expressed in smart contracts. Shares will be tokens or cryptoassets deployed on a community blockchain. At the moment, the community is trying to tokenize companies created under the traditional system. The companies of the future will be created directly on a market blockchain, that is, they will be born tokenized.

Tokens will eventually replace much of the traditional share system and the markets where shares are traded. The Internet Revolution will require fewer intermediaries and will be cheaper, more universal, and more efficient. The blockchain itself will publicly report the creation of commercial companies. Anyone in the world will have the option of becoming a partner in a company created under the blockchain system. They will only have to connect their wallet and contribute cryptoassets.

Likewise, the contracts entered into by the company will be made directly on the blockchain itself. These contracting systems will reduce many cases of rogue traders, deceit, and theft, in part because assets, rights, and obligations will be anchored on-chain and auditable by the community.

In the new Internet corporate law, capital increases and reductions, mergers, acquisitions, and spin-offs will be executed on the blockchain in a matter of seconds. The agility, universality, and cost reduction of this legal system will render many modern registry and legal systems inoperative. These will be nostalgically studied and remembered in legal history books.

Moreover, in the Internet legal system, a good reputation will have more value. With the Internet Revolution, we will witness the tokenization of honor. Reputation will not be a vague social impression. It will be reinforced through on-chain history, verifiable attestations, and repeated performance in markets where counterparties can switch away with a click. Something like this is already happening in the reviews and reputational signals that users post across the Internet.

The "society of good reputation" was a central legal figure that emerged in Islamic commercial practice. Merchants formed societies without capital, because what mattered was their good name. It was also called the "partnership of the penniless" (sharika al-mafalis), created when two people formed a partnership in order to buy and sell without capital. In these partnerships, capital consisted of reputation and status, and credit was extended only to the one with good standing among the people[288].

Thus, in the legal system of the Internet, reliable business will be done only with companies created on blockchain that have a good reputation, which will be even more valuable than it is today. As Pierre Bourdieu pointed out, describing a similar economy based on trust: "it is quite possible to turn honor into money, but almost impossible to turn money into honor"[289].

Merchant contracts concluded on blockchain will be executed from the blockchain itself. In some simple cases, such as escrow contracts or international payments, everything will be automatic, without third-

---

[288] Sarakhsi in Udovitch, 1975:11.

[289] Graeber, D. (2011). Debt: The First 5,000 Years. Kindle edition.

party intervention. In other cases, the intervention of third parties, called “oracles” in blockchain jargon, will be required. They will confirm data, report that events have taken place, or attest to facts such as the delivery of goods in good condition. These legal oracles will compete on accuracy and integrity, because their future business will depend on reputation, incentives, and the consequences of being wrong.

This is why new public authenticators will emerge, who will not waste time legitimizing signatures or accrediting identities in the old way, since those elements can be recorded on-chain. The new public authenticators will be chosen from the community itself for their trust and authority. A Brazilian national could confirm an agreement between a Spaniard and an Australian regarding delivery in Hong Kong. This system will not be based on place, as it is today.

The law of the Industrial Revolution was based on localism, centralism, and bureaucracy. Internet law is based on decentralization, universality, and efficiency. The Internet Legal Revolution will modify, through its community, the traditional registry and notary public system.

The community itself, aware of the power of the technology, will promote and implement the new legal system. States will have no choice but to adapt.

Ultimately, I believe that the true regulation of new technologies can only come from the community itself. It is the community that must incorporate into its own digital law (blockchain or distributed ledger technology) effective justice mechanisms, along with the requirement for fair and effective standards. It is the community itself that can demand compliance requirements in order for other users to participate.

Just as a wallet user must be responsible for safeguarding private keys and not entrust them to a third party, the community must also be responsible and accept that only it can regulate appropriate solutions through its own technology, without delegating that function to third parties.

Only in this way can the new law of the Internet be built.

7. Main Digital Laws of Internet Jurisdiction

7.1. Bitcoin Digital Law

Digital Laws often begin with an explanatory memorandum, usually a whitepaper that explains the problem, the proposed rules, and the incentive structure. In Bitcoin's case, that memorandum is Satoshi Nakamoto's whitepaper[290].

The Bitcoin Digital Law is not written on paper. It is programmed in open-source software and deployed on the internet through GitHub, a code-hosting service used for collaborative development. In practical terms, the repository functions like a living statute book: it shows the rules, the history of changes, and the discussion around proposed updates. The code is publicly available at GitHub.

To make the system easier to understand for a legal audience, I have rewritten this Digital Law in Annex 1 as if it were a traditional statute. From that text, we can deduce that Bitcoin operates as digital law.

The Digital Law contains: the objective scope of application in Internet Jurisdiction (Article 1); the governing principles of immutability, decentralization, and security (Article 1, paragraph 4); the subjective scope under the principle of nondiscrimination (Article 2); sovereignty of the community (Article 3); limited

---

[290] Nakamoto, S. (2008). Bitcoin: A Peer-to-Peer Electronic Cash System (p. 1).

issuance of Bitcoins at 21 million (Article 4); divisibility of each Bitcoin (Article 5); the Bitcoin creation system (Article 6); the halving schedule (Article 7); the Bitcoin payment system (Article 8); and the rules for amending the Bitcoin Digital Law (Article 9).

Two aspects of this Digital Law deserve special attention.

First, Bitcoin solves the double-spending problem, often illustrated through the Byzantine Generals problem. Before Bitcoin, digital payments generally required a centralized intermediary, such as a bank, to prevent the same unit of digital value from being spent twice. Bitcoin proposes a peer-to-peer solution by time-stamping transactions in a proof-of-work chain, creating a record that cannot be rewritten without overwhelming network consensus.

As the whitepaper explains, participants need a shared history of transactions, so that "transactions have to be publicly announced.[291]" In short, Bitcoin's ledger is public, replicated, and continuously validated by the network.

Bitcoin's proof-of-work consensus mechanism (Article 6, paragraphs 2 and 5, and Article 8) closes a new block roughly every 10 minutes. Miners compete to find a nonce that makes the block header hash fall below a target threshold (the network difficulty)[292].

---

[291] The whitepaper can be read here: https://bitcoin.org/bitcoin.pdf

[292] The miner must find a nonce such that SHA-256(block header + nonce) produces a number less than the target (difficulty).

Once a valid block is found, other nodes verify it and extend the chain.

Simplified rule: SHA-256(block header + nonce) < target.

Key terms: Block header (transaction summary, prior block hash, timestamp, and other data); nonce (a number miners vary); SHA-256 (the hash function used by Bitcoin); target (the difficulty threshold that is periodically adjusted).

Why it matters: finding a valid nonce is computationally expensive, but verifying the result is quick. This asymmetry is what makes proof-of-work secure in practice.

The Byzantine Generals scenario, often described today as a 51% attack, occurs when an adversary controls a majority of the network's hashing power and attempts to build an alternative history. In Bitcoin, the chain with the most accumulated proof-of-work is treated as authoritative. The larger and more distributed the network becomes, the more costly and impractical such an attack is to execute.

Second, Bitcoin is designed as a deflationary digital currency. The total supply is capped at 21 million Bitcoins (Article 4), and the last fraction is projected to be mined around the year 2140 (Article 7). Each Bitcoin is divisible into 100,000,000 units called satoshis[293] (Article 5). This divisibility matters because it allows

---

[293] 100,000,000 satoshis = 1 Bitcoin.

Bitcoin to function in everyday payments even if one full Bitcoin becomes expensive.

Miners are incentivized to support the network, validate transactions, and secure the system because successful mining is rewarded with newly issued Bitcoin plus transaction fees. This incentive alignment is often described through game theory[294]. For an attacker, the economically rational path is usually to support the network rather than undermine it, since the value of the reward depends on the network's credibility. In the early days of Bitcoin, many computer scientists tried to attack the network, and when they realized it was impossible, they became miners[295].

I discussed halving in Chapter 2. At each halving event, the block subsidy paid to miners is cut in half (Article 7). Historically, miners respond by improving efficiency, exiting if they cannot operate profitably, and relying more on transaction fees and price appreciation over time.

A symbolic detail reinforces Bitcoin's monetary critique. In the genesis block, Nakamoto embedded a headline from The Times: "The Times 03/Jan/2009 Chancellor on brink of second bailout for banks." This has been widely read as a signal that Bitcoin was

---

[294] Incentive alignment and game theory are used throughout later Digital Laws, including DeFi protocols that reward participation through staking, liquidity mining, and fee sharing.

[295] For a narrative of Bitcoin's early community, see Popper, N. (2015). Digital Gold: Bitcoin and the Inside Story of the Misfits and Millionaires Trying to Reinvent Money.

designed as money insulated from discretionary monetary policy.

Finally, I would like to highlight the work of computer scientist, cryptographer, and legal theorist Nick Szabo. He pioneered the concept of smart contracts in the 1990s, describing them as mechanisms that can facilitate, verify, or enforce agreements without relying on intermediaries. Smart contracts later became foundational for platforms such as Ethereum and other virtual-machine blockchains.

Szabo is often associated with Ethereum, but his influence on Bitcoin is also significant. In 1998, he described "Bit Gold," one of the most relevant conceptual predecessors to Bitcoin. Although never implemented, Bit Gold anticipated several elements later used by Bitcoin, including proof-of-work, chained records, and the removal of trusted intermediaries.

From 1997 to 2002, Szabo published several articles that remain useful for understanding Bitcoin's design logic:

- "The God Protocols"[296] (1997), which explores mutually confidential auditing protocols for verifying transaction logs and consistency.
- "Trusted Third Parties are Security Holes"[297] (2001), which explains how intermediaries can

[296] https://nakamotoinstitute.org/library/the-god-protocols/

[297] https://nakamotoinstitute.org/library/trusted-third-parties/

become system vulnerabilities, and why removing them improves resilience.

- "Origins of Money"[298] (2002), which explores non-fiduciary money and the social functions that make money durable outside state issuance.

7.2. Ethereum Digital Law

Ethereum Digital Law is more complex than Bitcoin's. Vitalik Buterin realized that a blockchain could do more than issue and transfer a currency. It could also support decentralized applications, or Dapps, through programmable smart contracts.

The wording of the Ethereum Digital Law is attached as Annex 2. It reflects the current version, given that the community has modified Ethereum's rules multiple times, including major protocol upgrades. Ethereum regulates its objective scope and application in Internet Jurisdiction (Article 1). The network's governing principles include decentralization, openness with flexibility, and cryptographic security (Article 1, paragraph 4).

Ethereum employs a Turing-complete virtual machine (EVM)[299] (Article 10). Developers can write and deploy smart contracts, meaning self-executing code that can manage and transfer digital assets,

---

[298] https://econwpa.ub.uni-muenchen.de/econ-wp/eh/papers/0211/0211005.html

[299] A Turing-complete virtual machine can execute any algorithm given enough time and resources. In blockchain contexts, this describes smart-contract platforms capable of running general-purpose programs.

register and execute agreements, and automate complex conditions. This is the core legal difference from Bitcoin: Ethereum is designed as a general-purpose platform for issuing additional Digital Laws.

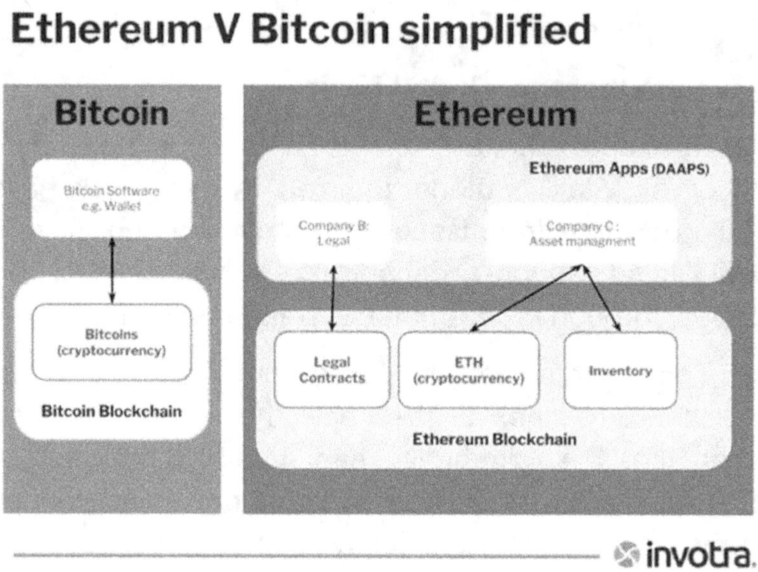

Figure 14. This graph reflects the base regulatory difference between Bitcoin and Ethereum.

Unlike Bitcoin, Ether does not have a fixed maximum supply (Article 4). Ether is divisible to 18 decimal places (Article 5). Ethereum originally used proof-of-work, but the community adopted a major change through Ethereum Improvement Proposal (EIP) 3675 (Article 8), transitioning to proof-of-stake

(Article 7)[300]. This shift, commonly called "The Merge," replaced energy-intensive mining with validator staking and changed how the network secures consensus.

Article 2 regulates subjective scope and nondiscrimination. Anyone can participate in the network and, in that sense, anyone can legislate from Ethereum by deploying their own smart contracts or issuing their own tokens.

Many websites provide user-friendly interfaces that generate standard token contracts, such as ERC-20 tokens. For example, this page offers a guided workflow: https://smithii.io/create-token-erc20-ethereum/. These tools can be convenient, but convenience also increases risk. A token contract should be reviewed, tested, and, where possible, independently audited before it is used by the public.

A blockchain is typically accessed through a wallet. One of the best known is MetaMask. It can be added to a browser or used on mobile. Many tutorials on YouTube explain how to operate this wallet.

A token can be created for many purposes, such as customer loyalty programs, governance, or access to a service. Key design choices include the token name, total supply, whether additional issuance is possible, whether there is a cap, whether airdrops will

300 EIP-3675 formalizes Ethereum's transition from proof of work to proof of stake and the required changes to disable PoW and migrate to the Beacon Chain.

be used, and how rights or benefits are tied to token ownership.

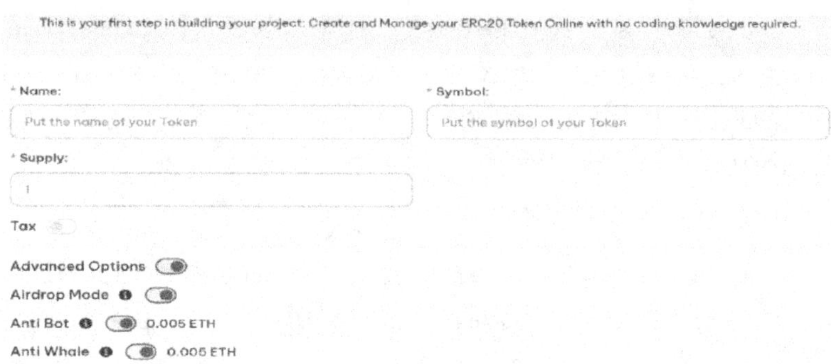

Figure 15. Example of information to fill in to create a token.

A notable early Digital Law issued on Ethereum was CryptoKitties, released in November 2017. CryptoKitties allowed users to collect, breed, and trade unique digital cats represented as non-fungible tokens (NFTs), using the ERC-721 standard.

Demand became so intense that it congested Ethereum's network, revealing how quickly a successful application can stress a public blockchain.

A one-euro coin is fungible: it has the same value regardless of who holds it. An NFT is non-fungible: each token is unique and therefore not interchangeable in the same way, like a specific painting. Other well-known applications associated with Ethereum include Axie Infinity and Decentraland.

Initial Coin Offerings (ICOs) were also prominent on Ethereum in 2017 and 2018. Fundraising could occur based on a whitepaper and marketing, sometimes without a minimum viable product.

The total amount raised was in the billions of US dollars, and at least 50% of ICOs from that period are widely viewed as failures [301]. Two widely cited examples are EOS, which raised about $4.2 billion[302], and Tezos, which raised about $232 million[303].

This episode shows both the power of permissionless fundraising and the downside of weak due diligence, where hype can substitute for governance, product, and accountability.

Ethereum has also been instrumental in the rise of decentralized finance (DeFi), enabling financial services without traditional intermediaries. Common DeFi categories include lending, decentralized exchanges, liquidity protocols, staking, yield strategies, and stablecoin issuance.

Finally, DAOs (decentralized autonomous organizations) proliferated on Ethereum. They enable collective decision-making and automated execution through smart contracts, without a centralized

---

[301] Walters, S. (March 30, 2023). Nearly 50% of ICOs from 2017 Are Failing. Coin Bureau. https://coinbureau.com/analysis/icos-from-2017-failing-heres-why/

[302] Kaur, G. (February 17, 2024). What is EOS? Cointelegraph. https://es.cointelegraph.com/learn/what-is-eos

[303] Bastardo, J. (July 13, 2017). Tezos breaks ICO fundraising record. Criptonoticias. https://www.criptonoticias.com/mercados/tezos-rompe-record-recaudacion-ico-232-millones-financiamiento/

authority. Early examples include MakerDAO (issued in 2015)[304] and The DAO (launched in 2016)[305].

In the wake of Ethereum, other smart-contract platforms emerged to compete on cost, speed, scalability, and developer experience. Notable examples include Binance Smart Chain (BSC), Polkadot, Cardano, Solana, Avalanche, Tezos, NEO, Fantom, Algorand, and Cosmos. These networks launched at different times and reflect different tradeoffs among decentralization, security, governance, and performance.

Figure 16. CryptoKitties. Source: https://www.code-brew.com/

Layer 2 solutions have also emerged on Ethereum. They are built on top of Ethereum and aim to reduce

---

304 MakerDAO issues the stablecoin DAI and governance token MKR through a protocol implemented on Ethereum.

305 The DAO was a decentralized investment organization launched in 2016 that suffered an exploit, leading to a hard fork and the creation of Ethereum Classic.

congestion, lower transaction fees, and increase speed without compromising the security of the base layer.

One of the best known is Polygon (formerly Matic), which launched as Matic in 2017 and later rebranded as Polygon. Like Polygon, many other Layer 2 systems have emerged, including optimistic rollups and zero-knowledge rollups.

7.3. Digital Laws related to Decentralized Finance (DeFi)

One of the most relevant Digital Laws in decentralized finance is Uniswap, issued in November 2018.

Uniswap is a decentralized exchange (DEX) that allows users to swap tokens directly from their own wallets without relying on a centralized intermediary (Article 1). Rather than matching buyers and sellers through an order book, Uniswap uses an automated market maker (AMM) model that prices trades based on liquidity in smart-contract pools.

Uniswap creates liquidity pools that hold token pairs. Anyone can create a pool by depositing two assets of equal value, such as ETH and WBTC[306]. Once a pool exists, other users can contribute additional liquidity by depositing the same pair in the correct ratio. In return, liquidity providers receive LP

306 Wrapped Bitcoin (WBTC) is an ERC-20 token on Ethereum designed to represent BTC 1:1, enabling Bitcoin liquidity to be used in Ethereum-based DeFi applications.

tokens that represent their share of the pool (Article 2, paragraph 2).

Liquidity providers earn a portion of the trading fee, historically 0.30% on many pools, shared among providers in proportion to their liquidity (Article 4, paragraph 3).

A key risk is impermanent loss (Article 6.2). Pool prices adjust algorithmically based on supply and demand. A simplified model uses the constant-product formula $x \times y = k$ (Article 4, paragraph 2), where x and y are the token quantities in the pool and k remains constant unless liquidity is added or removed.

Users retain custody of their assets because Uniswap does not hold funds. Swaps and pool operations are executed by smart contracts under the Ethereum Virtual Machine (Article 1, paragraph 3). Users also pay gas fees, which can rise during congestion. Ethereum's Digital Law (Annex 2) regulates this type of expenditure.

"UNI" is Uniswap's governance token (Article 5), launched in September 2020. UNI holders can vote on protocol changes, including fee settings, incentive programs, and upgrades.

Because listing is permissionless, new tokens can be traded quickly, but that openness also enables scams. Users must verify contract addresses, token symbols, and liquidity sources because impostor tokens can imitate legitimate projects.

From a regulatory standpoint, DEX activity raises challenges for compliance systems designed around centralized intermediaries, including controls related to financial surveillance and anti-money laundering frameworks.

Other important DeFi Digital Laws include Aave (decentralized lending and borrowing, including flash loans), MakerDAO (stablecoin issuance through collateralized positions), Compound (algorithmic interest rates for lending markets), Curve (efficient stablecoin swaps), and SushiSwap (a Uniswap fork that expanded into yield strategies, staking, and token launches).

The SushiSwap fork is one of the most controversial and instructive episodes in DeFi history. In August 2020, SushiSwap offered incentives by distributing its SUSHI token to Uniswap liquidity providers. Those providers deposited their Uniswap LP tokens into SushiSwap to earn additional rewards, a strategy often described as a "vampire attack."

After SushiSwap accumulated a large amount of Uniswap liquidity, it migrated that liquidity to its own pools, moving more than $1 billion in value on September 9, 2020.

Uniswap responded by launching the UNI governance token on September 17, 2020, and retroactively distributing tokens to prior users, which helped regain liquidity and community support. This episode illustrates how token incentives can shift market structure quickly, and why governance design, distribution, and community alignment are not secondary features but core components of a DeFi protocol's stability.

Yearn Finance introduced automated strategies that search for and route deposits to the highest-yield opportunities across DeFi. Its creator, André Cronje, automated yield optimization and popularized the idea of "vaults" that manage strategy execution on behalf of users. For a period, the Yearn token (YFI) traded at a higher unit price than Bitcoin, highlighting how market narratives can amplify scarce governance tokens.

Balancer enables AMM pools with customizable asset weightings rather than a strict 50/50 ratio. Synthetix issues synthetic assets that track real-world prices, including fiat currencies, commodities, and equities, using collateral and oracle pricing.

Each blockchain tends to have multiple DEX ecosystems. Ethereum has Uniswap and SushiSwap; Binance Smart Chain (BSC) has PancakeSwap and BakerySwap; Avalanche has Trader Joe and Pangolin; Solana has Serum and Raydium; and Polygon supports QuickSwap and SushiSwap, among others[307].

---

[307] Examples continue across ecosystems, including Fantom (SpookySwap, SpiritSwap), Arbitrum (Uniswap, SushiSwap), Optimism (Uniswap, Velodrome), Tezos (Quipuswap), and others.

7.4. Digital Laws related to stablecoins

Stablecoins are cryptoassets designed to maintain a stable value by linking to an external reference, such as the US dollar or gold. Their role is important because they reduce the volatility common in many cryptocurrencies and make pricing, settlement, and collateralization more practical.

Stablecoins differ mainly by the mechanism used to maintain their peg:

1. **Fiat-backed stablecoins**. These are backed by reserves of a fiat currency held with a custodian. Examples include USDT (Tether)[308] and USDC. These are not decentralized because they depend on a central issuer and the integrity of its reserves.

2. **Crypto-collateralized stablecoins**. The best-known example is DAI, issued through MakerDAO. Any user can create DAI by locking crypto collateral such as ETH. Overcollateralization is typically required to manage volatility, and issuance is governed by smart contracts on Ethereum.

3. **Algorithmic stablecoins**. These attempt to maintain a peg through supply and demand algorithms rather than direct collateral. The most striking example is TerraUSD (UST), which collapsed in May 2022, as discussed in Chapter 1.

---

[308] See Chapter 1 for a fuller discussion of Tether and the role of centralized issuers in stablecoin markets.

4. **Commodity-backed stablecoins**. These are linked to physical assets such as gold or real estate. Examples include PAX Gold (PAXG) and Tether Gold (XAUT), which are marketed as being backed by allocated gold.

It is not the object of this work to list every Digital Law, since more than 2.5 million cryptoassets have been issued. Instead, I will mention additional categories that support the growth and functioning of the community.

First, oracle protocols. Oracles provide blockchains with external data, such as price feeds, interest rates, or real-world events. Chainlink is one of the best-known oracle systems, alongside Band Protocol and UMA. Because blockchains are difficult to attack directly, many exploits focus on oracle manipulation or corrupted inputs[309].

Second, scalability protocols aim to increase throughput without sacrificing decentralization or security. Examples include the Lightning Network for Bitcoin and Layer 2 systems on Ethereum, such as optimistic rollups and zk-rollups.

Third, interoperability protocols facilitate communication among blockchains, including Polkadot, Cosmos, and Wanchain.

---

[309] One characteristic exploit is the flash-loan attack, often combined with price-oracle manipulation. See: https://www.welivesecurity.com/la-es/2023/01/26/que-es-ataque-flash-loan-prestamo-rapido-plataformas-defi/

Finally, privacy protocols such as Monero, Zcash, and Tornado Cash enable anonymous or more private transactions. These tools create obvious tensions with regulatory frameworks related to anti-money laundering compliance and tax enforcement.

As the community becomes more aware of this new way of regulating and organizing society, it will propose more valuable and serious solutions. It is up to the community to seek and offer solutions, including legal solutions, to the regulatory challenges of the future.

It is also up to the community to reflect on its own identity and situation so that it can offer solutions consistent with the new digital reality. In short, the community must mature. Rather than waiting for the State to define every answer, Internet Jurisdiction invites the community to build standards, dispute-resolution mechanisms, and trustworthy institutions that match the technology's decentralized structure.

Let us take advantage of the power that Satoshi introduced: the ability to transmit value and information as equals. Even if change brings discomfort, it also offers a chance to reclaim sovereignty and build a more honest architecture for cooperation. Let us make the most of this unique moment in history.

ANNEXES

Annex 1: Bitcoin Digital Law

Article 1: Intended Scope

1. This Digital Law is applicable in the Internet Jurisdiction and regulates the issuance and operation of the digital currency called "Bitcoin".

2. This payment system is based on peer-to-peer relationships and therefore lacks central entities.

3. The Bitcoin community is not subject to distinctions of race, nationality, borders, or other typical state divisions. Bitcoin's jurisdiction is the Internet, where there are no political or geographic barriers. The Bitcoin network is global, and its operation is based on decentralization and autonomy in which state regulations have no direct relevance to use and participation in the network. Participants are treated equally, regardless of location or status, which guarantees neutrality in operations.

4. Principles governing the Bitcoin payment network:

a) Immutability: When a transaction is included in a block and that block is added to the blockchain, the transaction becomes part of a permanent and unalterable record. The blockchain structure links each block to the previous one, creating a chronological chain that cannot be modified without redoing all subsequent blocks, which is practically impossible under decentralized consensus.

b) Decentralization: The Bitcoin network operates on a decentralized network of nodes, which means there is no central authority that can intervene in or modify a transaction once it has been confirmed.

c) Cryptographic security: The cryptography that secures each transaction and block is extremely robust. If someone attempted to reverse a transaction, they would need to control at least 51% of the network's mining power (a "51% attack"), which is highly unlikely given the network's scale and decentralization.

Article 2: Subjective Scope and Principle of Non-Discrimination

1. The payment system called "Bitcoin" is open to all persons in the world who have access to the Internet, regardless of age, income, tax or personal identification, marital status, nationality, race, sex, sexual orientation, political ideology, level of education, curriculum vitae, religion or beliefs, parentage, criminal record, personal abilities, disabilities, or any other subjective qualification or assessment. In this payment system, there is no discrimination for any of these reasons, guaranteeing free, barrier-free access.

2. To interact with the Bitcoin network, each user must use a public address, which serves as an identifier to receive and send funds. To access the funds associated with a public address, it is essential to have

a private key. The private key is strictly personal and gives absolute control over the bitcoins stored at that address. The holder of the private key has full control over the funds, and safeguarding the key is the responsibility of the user.

3. The Bitcoin network does not demand or require personal data, tax identification, or any form of prior information about the parties involved in a transaction. The system is pseudonymous by design, because transactions are linked only to public addresses. Transactions are public and visible on the blockchain, and each user controls their degree of exposure depending on how they manage keys and addresses.

Article 3: Community Sovereignty

1. The power of the Bitcoin blockchain rests with the community of users actively participating in the network, not with a central authority. Every participant in the network, through node operations, transaction validation, or system usage, is part of this community. Nodes validate transactions and blocks, ensuring transparency and legitimacy. In this way, the decentralized community supports and validates the rules governing the operation of the Bitcoin blockchain, consolidating a system of collective governance.

2. Because sovereignty rests with the community, any modification of these rules, as regulated in Article 9, can only be made through a consensus process. This consensus requires a significant majority of participating nodes in the network to agree to implement the change.

Article 4: Limited Issuance of Bitcoins

1. Bitcoin shall have a maximum issuance of 21 million units, with no possibility of creating more.

2. Each new bitcoin unit is issued through the mining process regulated in Article 6.

Article 5: Principle of Divisibility

1. Each Bitcoin can be divided into 100,000,000 smaller units, known as satoshis. Each satoshi represents 0.00000001 BTC. This divisibility allows Bitcoin to be used in transactions of any size, facilitating its use even when the value of a single Bitcoin is high.

2. Bitcoin's divisibility ensures that, despite the limited issuance of 21 million units, small and precise transactions can always be made. This principle is crucial to the functionality and adoption of Bitcoin as a global digital currency, allowing users to perform low-value transactions and micropayments without friction.

Article 6: System for the Creation of Bitcoins

1. New bitcoins may be created until the 21 million units referred to in Article 4 have been issued.

2. Bitcoins are issued through a mining process that validates transaction blocks through a decentralized network of nodes. This process is codified in the Bitcoin protocol and uses a consensus mechanism known as Proof of Work, as regulated in paragraph 5 of this Article.

3. The creation of new bitcoins follows the principle of progressive reward reduction, known as halving. Approximately every 4 years, the reward received by miners for adding a new block to the blockchain is reduced by half. This mechanism ensures that the issuance rate decreases over time until the total issuance reaches 21 million bitcoins.

4. Once the 21 million bitcoins have been issued, no more new coins will be generated. At that point, miners will be incentivized solely through transaction fees paid by users to process transactions.

5. The Bitcoin network protects the process of creating new coins and validating transactions through advanced cryptography based on the SHA-256 hashing algorithm. Miners compete by solving complex computational problems (Proof of Work) to add new blocks to the ledger (blockchain), ensuring the security and integrity of the system. These problems are solved in an average time of 10 minutes per block, maintaining a predictable pace of transaction validation and coin issuance according to the protocol. This design keeps the network robust and resistant to attack, while miners are incentivized through newly issued bitcoins and transaction fees.

Article 7: Halving

Halving occurs every 210,000 blocks mined, which translates to an approximate 4-year interval. At each halving, the reward miners receive for adding a new block to the blockchain is reduced by half.

From the first block called “genesis,” the mining reward is 50 BTC. This amount is halved at each halving, for example to 25 BTC at the first halving, 12.5 BTC at the second, 6.25 BTC at the third, and so on until the reward reaches 0.00000001 BTC (1 satoshi), scheduled for the penultimate halving in 2136. The last halving is expected in 2140, at which point there will be no more mining rewards.

Article 8: Bitcoin Network Payment System

1. Bitcoin is a payment system based on the transfer of bitcoins created in accordance with Article 6. Transactions are grouped into blocks that are processed and confirmed by miners. Miners compete to solve complex mathematical problems through Proof of Work. Once solved, the block is added to the blockchain, ensuring the immutability and security of transactions.

2. Under the original protocol rules, each block has a base size limit of 1 megabyte (MB), which allows a set of transactions to be included. In practice, modern block weight rules can allow effective capacity above 1 MB for certain transactions, while still preserving the protocol’s constraints on resource use.

Article 9: Amendments to the Regulation of this Law

1. Any modification to the Bitcoin protocol, including rules regarding coin issuance, must be proposed through a public mechanism for improvement proposals known as Bitcoin Improvement Proposals (BIPs). These proposals must be approved through broad community consensus, reflected in adoption by

nodes running the network and miners processing transactions.

2. While Bitcoin is resistant to arbitrary change, updates to the protocol can be implemented when broad consensus is reached within the community. Modifications that do not reach consensus may result in a fork of the blockchain, creating two protocol versions that can coexist.

3. If a significant part of the network sought to change the protocol rules, but another part opposed the change, a blockchain fork could occur. In that case, two different versions of Bitcoin would be created: one maintaining the original rules and another implementing the modified rules.

Annex 2: Ethereum Digital Law

Updated and current version according to the latest reforms approved by the Ethereum community.

Article 1: Intended Scope

1. This Digital Law is applicable in the Internet Jurisdiction and regulates the operation and issuance of the decentralized platform called Ethereum and its native cryptoasset, Ether (ETH).

2. The Ethereum platform enables the development of decentralized applications (dApps) through smart contracts. These dApps run on the Ethereum Virtual Machine (EVM), enabling automation and autonomous execution of agreements without intermediaries.

3. Ethereum's system is based on peer-to-peer relationships and smart contracts, lacking central entities that manage or control transactions or decentralized applications. Ethereum is a global, decentralized network with no political or geographic barriers.

4. Principles governing the Ethereum network:

a) Decentralization: The Ethereum network operates on a distributed network of nodes that validate transactions and execute smart contracts, ensuring no central authority controls the network.

b) Openness and flexibility: Ethereum allows developers to create smart contracts and decentralized applications for a wide variety of use cases, from financial systems to games and social networks.

c) Cryptographic security: Ethereum uses advanced cryptography to protect transactions, smart contracts, and user data recorded on the blockchain.

Note: Ethereum's transition from Proof of Work (PoW) to Proof of Stake (PoS), known as "The Merge," was implemented through several Ethereum Improvement Proposals (EIPs), including EIP-3675, EIP-4345, and EIP-4399.

Article 2: Subjective Scope and Principle of Non-Discrimination

1. Everyone in the world with access to the Internet can interact with Ethereum, regardless of age, tax or personal identification, income, nationality, or similar criteria. Access is free and without barriers.

2. To use Ethereum, users generate a public address and a private key, which serve as unique identifiers to access funds or execute smart contracts. The private key grants absolute control over resources stored at that address, and it is the user's responsibility to protect it.

3. Ethereum does not demand or require personal data, tax identification, or any other information about participants. Transactions and smart contracts are pseudonymous because they are linked only to public addresses. The information is public and visible on the blockchain.

Article 3: Sovereignty of the Ethereum Community

1. The power of the Ethereum blockchain rests with the community of users who actively participate in the network by operating nodes and validating transactions. The community supports and validates the rules governing the operation of the Ethereum blockchain.

2. Any modification to Ethereum's rules, as regulated in Article 8, can only be made through a consensus process within the community. For this purpose, improvement proposals known as Ethereum Improvement Proposals (EIPs) are used.

Article 4: Issuance of Ether

1. There is no fixed cap on the issuance of Ether. A fee-burning mechanism reduces net issuance over time by burning a portion of transaction fees (for example, through the base-fee mechanism introduced in EIP-1559).

2. New Ether is issued as a reward for validators in the Proof of Stake (PoS) system, in accordance with Article 6.

Article 5: Principle of Divisibility of Ether

1. Ether (ETH) is divisible to 18 decimal places. The smallest unit is a wei (1 wei = 0.000000000000000001 ETH). This allows for extremely precise and low-value transactions.

Article 6: Creation of Ether

1. Ether is created through the Proof of Stake (PoS) consensus mechanism.

2. Validators secure the network and are rewarded with new Ether by validating blocks of transactions through the participation of their staked Ether in the consensus protocol.

Article 7: Proof of Stake (PoS)

Ethereum operates under the Proof of Stake consensus mechanism, whereby validators are selected to create blocks based on the amount of Ether they have staked, ensuring a more efficient and environmentally sustainable process than the original PoW system.

Article 8: Protocol Modifications

1. Modifications to the Ethereum protocol are proposed through Ethereum Improvement Proposals (EIPs), which are discussed and approved by the community and developers.

2. Forks may occur if there is disagreement over the implementation of certain changes.

Article 9: Platform for Creating dApps

1. Ethereum is a decentralized platform that enables the creation and execution of decentralized applications (dApps), alongside its payment system and smart contracts. Unlike traditional applications, dApps on Ethereum are executed in a decentralized

manner and do not rely on a central server or controlling entity.

2. Smart contracts are self-executing programs with predefined rules, written in code and stored on the Ethereum blockchain. These contracts are automatically triggered when conditions set in their code are met. Contract execution is immutable, transparent, and secure because it is verified through distributed consensus.

3. Transactions on Ethereum, including transactions that interact with smart contracts, are verified by network nodes. Nodes validate and ensure that interactions and contract execution follow the protocol rules.

4. dApps on Ethereum are developed using programming languages such as Solidity or Vyper.

5. Once deployed, a dApp cannot be modified unilaterally by a single entity, supporting predictable execution. Users can interact directly with dApps through interfaces that facilitate interaction with smart contracts on the blockchain.

6. All transactions and contract executions on Ethereum require payment of a gas fee in Ether (ETH), which compensates validators for the use of computational resources. Gas requirements vary depending on contract complexity and network congestion.

Article 10: Ethereum Virtual Machine (EVM)

1. The Ethereum Virtual Machine (EVM) is the execution environment that enables smart contracts and transactions to run on the Ethereum network. The EVM exists on every node in the network, ensuring contracts and transactions are executed in the same way regardless of which node processes them.

2. All Ethereum transactions, including payments and smart contract interactions, are processed by the EVM. The EVM ensures that contract rules are applied consistently, regardless of the location or node that executes them.

3. Smart contracts are written in high-level languages such as Solidity or Vyper and compiled into bytecode, which is the language executed by the EVM. The bytecode is executed on each node, ensuring predictable and consistent behavior across the network.

4. Execution in the EVM consumes gas, which is the cost in Ether associated with the use of computational resources. Gas limits resource usage to help prevent overload and reduce exposure to certain classes of malicious behavior.

5. The EVM's deterministic execution helps ensure that results are consistent across nodes and that transactions and contract state changes are recorded immutably on the blockchain.

6. Decentralization: The EVM is decentralized in its operation, meaning it does not depend on a single

entity or server. Anyone running an Ethereum node has a copy of the EVM and can execute smart contracts independently.

Annex 3: Uniswap Digital Law

Article 1: Intended Scope

1. This Digital Law is applicable in the Internet Jurisdiction and regulates the functioning of the decentralized exchange protocol called Uniswap, built under the Ethereum Digital Law.

2. Uniswap is a decentralized platform designed to enable the exchange of tokens on the Ethereum blockchain without intermediaries. The protocol uses an automated market maker (AMM) model that allows users to transact through liquidity pools managed by smart contracts rather than relying on traditional order books.

3. The platform has no centralized control. All asset exchanges and liquidity provision are facilitated by smart contracts that operate autonomously on the blockchain. This allows anyone with Internet access and Ethereum-compatible tokens to participate in asset exchange and liquidity provision without restrictions.

4. Principles governing the Uniswap platform:

a) Decentralization: There is no central authority managing exchange operations on Uniswap. Users interact directly with smart contracts, enabling an autonomous system without intermediaries.

b) Universal access: Anyone with Internet access and an Ethereum-compatible wallet can use Uniswap to exchange tokens or provide liquidity without identity verification or restrictive requirements.

c) Automatic liquidity: Users can add liquidity to token pairs through smart contracts, allowing exchanges to occur without requiring a direct counterparty at the time of the transaction.

d) Transparency and security: All transactions and activities on Uniswap are public and verifiable on the Ethereum blockchain, supporting transparency in exchanges and asset security.

Article 2: Subjective Scope and Principle of Non-Discrimination

1. Any person with Internet access and an Ethereum-compatible wallet may participate in Uniswap. No third-party identification or approval is required to exchange tokens or provide liquidity.

2. Users can provide liquidity to token pairs by depositing equivalent value amounts of two tokens into a smart contract. In return, they receive liquidity provider tokens (LP tokens), which represent their share of the liquidity pool.

3. Liquidity providers can withdraw funds at any time by redeeming LP tokens for the underlying tokens in proportion to their share of the pool, along with a proportionate share of fees generated.

Article 3: Creating a Liquidity Pool in Uniswap

1. Any person may create a new liquidity pool on Uniswap, provided they have two Ethereum-compatible tokens and an initial amount to deposit into the pool. No permission from a central authority or intermediary platform is required.

2. To create a new pool, the user specifies the pair of tokens and provides an initial amount of both tokens to establish the liquidity reserve. This initial deposit determines the relative price of the tokens at that time, as Uniswap uses an automated market-making mechanism (AMM) based on the formula set out in Article 4.

3. Once the pool is created, any other user can contribute additional liquidity under the rules of Article 2. The pool creator has no special advantages over other liquidity providers and participates on equal terms.

4. Newly created pools may attract more participants depending on demand for the token pair and the fees generated by transactions.

Article 4: Operation of the Automated Market Maker (AMM) Exchange

1. Uniswap uses an Automated Market Maker (AMM) model that allows users to exchange tokens without an order book. Token prices are algorithmically determined based on the amounts of tokens available in each liquidity pool.

2. Token prices are calculated according to the equilibrium formula $x \times y = k$, where:

x: the quantity of the first token in the pool.

y: the quantity of the second token in the pool.

k: the invariant constant (product constant) that remains fixed at all times as long as no liquidity is added to or withdrawn from the pool.

This constant product model means that any transaction must be executed so that the product of x and y remains constant. As the quantity of one token increases in the pool, the quantity of the other token decreases to maintain equilibrium.

Article 5: Protocol Governance

1. Governance of Uniswap is exercised by UNI token holders, who can participate in decisions related to the future of the protocol.

2. Changes and improvements to Uniswap are proposed through Uniswap Improvement Proposals (UIP), which are voted on by UNI holders. UNI holders may propose modifications such as protocol updates, changes in transaction fees, or allocation of funds for development initiatives.

3. Proposals require a minimum level of participation and approval to pass. Quorum and voting requirements are established in the Uniswap governance rules to help ensure decisions are representative of the community.

Article 6: Security and Risks

1. Uniswap smart contracts are open source and have been audited. However, users should remain aware of risks, including potential vulnerabilities or implementation flaws.

2. Risk of impermanent loss: Liquidity providers may face impermanent losses when the prices of deposited tokens fluctuate significantly relative to the time of deposit. This can occur when the pool's token values change in a way that differs from simply holding the tokens outside of Uniswap.

3. Because Uniswap relies on the Ethereum network, functionality may be affected by scalability limitations, high gas fees, or Ethereum network disruptions.

www.ingramcontent.com/pod-product-compliance
Lightning Source LLC
LaVergne TN
LVHW011523200926
848484LV00001B/126